THE
WRITER
ON
HER WORK

VOLUME
II

EDITED AND WITH AN
INTRODUCTION
BY

JANET
STERNBURG

W·W·NORTON & COMPANY

NEW YORK·LONDON

THE

WRITER

ON

HER WORK

VOLUME

II

NEW ESSAYS IN
NEW TERRITORY

First published as a Norton paperback 1992

The text of this book is composed in Bembo,
with the display set in Corvinus Skyline and Bodoni.
Composition and manufacturing by The Haddon Craftsmen Inc.
Book design by Antonina Krass.

Library of Congress Cataloging-in-Publication Data

(Revised for vol. 2)

The writer on her work.

Vol. 2 has subtitle: New essays in new territory.

1. Women authors, American—Biography. 2. Authors,
American—20th century—Biography. 3. Authorship.
I. Sternburg, Janet.
PS151.W7 1980   810.9′9287   80–13613

ISBN 0–393–30867–7

W.W. Norton & Company, Inc., 500 Fifth Avenue, New York, N.Y. 10110
W.W. Norton & Company, Ltd., 10 Coptic Street, London WC1A 1PU

2 3 4 5 6 7 8 9 0

I write these thanks at a time in my life when I have every reason to be grateful to many people: to my husband, Steven Lavine, for the joy and partnership our marriage brings; to my parents, Helen and Sydney Sternburg, for the example of their resilience and kindness; to my friends Barbara Abrash, Perry Miller Adato, Karen Buck, Phyllis Chinlund, Nadine Covert, Prudence Crowther, Peggy Daniel, Mary Feldbauer Jansen, Bette Korman, James Lapine, Honor Moore, Susan Butler Plum, Karen Sacks, Aviva Slesin, Melinda Ward, and Ray Witlin, with a special salute to the members of the "chemo brigade" for their sustaining presence. I also want to thank Marcia Decker and Margaret Robe for their assistance; the Blue Mountain Center and the Djerassi Foundation for providing me with time and space; my agent, Gail Hochman; and my editor on both volumes, Carol Houck Smith, for her support and help, as well as for her gift of combining professional wisdom with friendship.

CONTENTS

CONTENTS

CONTENTS

NEW ESSAYS IN NEW TERRITORY: AN INTRODUCTION

JANET STERNBURG

As I write this introduction, I come upon a line that I scribbled on a yellow pad when I was working with each of the writers on revising her essay. "What an interesting group of people!" I noted to myself then, as a reminder to mention this rich array. I think now of the contributors: of, among others, Harriet Doerr, who published her first novel when she was in her seventies and who recently sent me a letter telling of new writing and posing the rhetorical question, "What would idle old age be like?" I think, too, of Jan Morris, once a man with a shelf of books under her earlier identity as James, and now a woman whose books go on multiplying; of Bharati Mukherjee, traveling from one continent to make her home in another and writing about the "unsettled magma between two worlds"; of Luisa Valenzuela, returning to her native Argentina after the fall of the military dictatorship and writing of "my need to touch the world with my own hands."

. . .

By appreciating the variety and depth of experience in these essays, I don't, of course, mean to correlate the fact of interesting lives with the ability to create literature. But my desire to elicit that range did inform the choices I made in commissioning the essays for this book, as did my admiration for the work of the individual authors. The diversity of writers suggests another hallmark: my intent has been to foster accounts in which the central themes of the making of one's work and one's self are refracted through personal sensibilities, and are expressed through the human, concrete particulars that are the materials of literature. The choices have been informed, too, by my decision to include writers from abroad as well as from the United States, with the hope that multiple voices, side by side, will suggest how the commonalities of women's experience can only become richer through the cross-fertilization of differences.

A decade ago, I went looking for a book that would tell me about how other women came to write, and how they saw their lives and their work. To my suprise then, difficult though it is to believe now, no such book existed. The first volume of *The Writer on Her Work* (1980) began, as I said in my earlier introduction, because "I needed to read it." Those essays, seen as a whole, took us inside a room of one's own as it is inhabited by writers of our time. During the intervening ten years, writing by women has been widely recognized, discussed, and celebrated. A room of one's own can now be seen as the first territory—hard won, cherished, and of abiding value. While the struggle to reach the room continues to be arduous for many women throughout the world, particularly when hindrances are imposed by circumstances of race, class, and economic position, I believe that we can look at the recent flourishing of creative work by women and say that the territory has, to a large extent, been claimed.

One consequence for this new book is that the narratives of the writers are different from those of the past and from what I expected. When I read through the first drafts as they were sent to me by their various authors, I began to recognize a direction to the change. The story of the struggle to become a writer was no longer at the core of many of these accounts. Instead, I found writers looking outward, embarked on a path of exploration through a terrain that is irregular and marked by fissures. In this collection, women are telling more expansive narratives, from different perspectives, about their engagement with the new territory that is the world.

In place of the search for wholeness which was a strong note sounded in the first volume, the writers here lay claim to the principle of transformation: to life's many processes of change, as well as to the writerly recognition of the protean qualities that lie, as Joy Williams says, "below the surface of a good story . . . accident, chaos, uncertainty—beautiful, shifting things." They write of the necessity to explore the mutable ground that lies between one culture and another, between oneself and others, as well as between a writer and her vocation.

A number of the writers here convey the experience of having been displaced by history, and the impact upon their writing of a life lived in several landscapes. "I write in order to belong," says Elena Poniatowska, in an account that takes her from the France of her upbringing to her mother's Mexico, a country previously lost to her when her family left during the Mexican Revolution. That hope of belonging can also become a claim: Mukherjee, crossing the distance between India and the United States, writes, "My literary agenda begins by acknowledging that America has transformed me. It does not end until I show how I (and the hundreds of thousands like me) have transformed America." In these pages, too, we are given images from the high Western European tradition, intensified for people sent into exile: Elizabeth Jolley evokes her father listening to Schubert *Lieder,* shading his hand over his eyes to hide tears. But these writers refuse the lure of nostalgia. Instead, with Mukherjee, they embrace as their subject "transformation—not preservation."

When Rita Dove asks, "How far can a Greek goddess lead a Black poet?" we see her taking on the task of finding the "missing link or, failing that, to invent it." With Poniatowska, we come to understand, too, that "one way of belonging was to listen, to see faces, to take them into oneself": in other words, by an act of imaginative empathy, to attempt to cross one's own borders. Several essays refer to the relationship of writer as witness, or scribe, or bridge between generations: conveyors all of the truths of others. Ursula Le Guin in her poem/essay taps the sources of world cultures; when she invokes Aphrodite the Maker, Spider Grandmother, and Coyote Woman, she is writing not to appropriate the cultures to which these references belong but rather to find kinship among an extensive range of understandings.

What relations are necessary, these essays ask, for a writer to belong to herself and also to others? In accounts of becoming a writer, one often encounters what Anne Tyler has called, in the first volume, a "setting-apart situation"—circumstances (loss, illness, or other isolating occurrences) that result in a child being estranged from what is taken to be normal life. That odd-feeling child is evoked in many of these essays. We see her alone, curled into a chair, set apart by an unappeasable longing for books that also serves to insulate her from other people's claims, a "strange bird" in Kaye Gibbons's words, searching for "a way to be." We also see her walking to school discovering, as Carolyn Forché does, that "strangeness was interesting," a means to heighten receptivity, to make a young writer porous to signs and stories.

This setting apart, so influential in a writer's childhood, acquires a different meaning for an adult. On the one hand, it remains necessary; writing requires solitude and a degree of estrangement from one's immediate surroundings. On the other hand, setting apart can be hazardous; it may also mean withdrawal from an equally necessary involvement with the currents of daily life. This dilemma of the creative life has long had particular meaning for women who have traditionally found it difficult to negotiate the relationship between *apart* and *a part.* There is such poignancy in these lines of Elizabeth Jolley's: "The best time for me to write is when people are sleeping. I am not needed in their dreams."

Lately, I have been rereading a relatively unknown memoir, *The Little Locksmith,* written by Katherine Butler Hathaway and published in the 1940s. How the book first entered my life many years ago I do not know, but I continue to be touched by its story of a young girl surmounting illness to discover independence and her vocation as a writer. One passage has especially moved me: "Although every serious person is expected to feel a responsibility toward his work as well as toward the people he loves, there is a point beyond which his devotion to his work cannot go without arousing the antagonism and jealousy of the people who love him and whom he loves. And, as everyone knows, Art is jealous too. This conflict can be as tragic as a civil war, because it is a war of the heart, between people who love each other." I find the quote particularly apt for this book not only because the writers here refer to the conflict but also because many of them describe the fray through the lens of time. In place of despair, they tell of the variety of strategies employed to put an end to that war of the heart, not by a victory, one side over the other, or even by the stalemate of a truce, but by the establishing of just relations.

In these essays, I discover too a new reckoning with the meaning of experience. Both Patricia Hampl and Carolyn Forché invoke the standard advice given to young writers: "Write what you know." But Forché warns against the old chestnut, hearing in it an implicit constraint, "you already know enough," that serves to keep one from venturing beyond safe limits. Hampl unlocks what she feels to be an underlying commandment, secret but potent—"write about what matters"—carrying with it an implicit charge to find out what does matter.

Constant here, and unswerving, is the writer's commitment to her vocation. It is reassuring to hear so practiced a writer as Margaret Atwood say, "It never gets any easier." Atwood also speaks of writing as a craft, one that is "acquired through the apprenticeship system, but you choose your own teachers." I would add that one also goes on choosing one's own "system." The writers in this book have made their vocations from paths they have hewn themselves. Their teachers include a variety of relations, among them mothers, daughters, grandmothers, husbands, friends, colleagues, remembered figures from the past, mentors urging one into one's future, as well as the writer's own self, reexamining and renewing her understandings.

Natalia Ginzburg recounts how, as a young woman, she saw a cart on the street one day bearing a mirror whose surface was tilted up to reflect sky and clouds. That image of the mirror initially evoked a vision of what might be possible, helping to release her from strictures she had placed upon herself and her writing. During a later period of difficulty, the mirror became dark to Ginzburg. But I believe that in the years that followed she let its metaphor deepen until it eventually reflected a view of art as compounded from a "mixture of pride, irony, physical tenderness, of imagination and memory, of clarity and obscurity." In place of a single image, however luminous it must once have been within its frame, we see instead the necessity for a more complex vision.

There is a sense in many of these essays of women comprehending themselves as amalgams of experiences, some that fit together in a clear trajectory, others that diverge or collide. *She tends to the plural,* writes Ursula Le Guin: *I, for example, am Ursula: Miss Ursula Kroeber/Mrs. then Ms. Le Guin;/Ursula K. Le Guin; this latter is/"the writer" but who were/who are, the others? She is the writer/ at their work.* There is a tone of playfulness here, a pleasure in sliding under the wire of definitions and in accepting life's revisions, that might not have been possible a decade or so ago. To me, that pleasure feels related to a relaxation that has been arrived at because hard-won changes of past years have allowed many women to shrug from their shoulders the burden of rigidly imposed identity.

This understanding of one's self as a fullness of many selves gives us a new plenitude. In answer to her question *What are they doing, these plurals of her?* Le Guin responds, I believe, for all the writers in this book:

> Her work, I really think her work
> is finding what her real work is
> and doing it
> her work, her own work
> her being human,
> her being in the world.

I chose to begin the first volume of *The Writer on Her Work* with a quote from Louise Bogan: "*In a time lacking in truth and certainty and filled with anguish and despair, no woman should be shamefaced in attempting to give back to the world, through her work, a portion of its lost heart.*" Now, ten years later, I think about how that quote seems especially prophetic for our current time. I think, too, about how this book, like the first volume, began because I needed to read it. Conscious of changes in my life and in the world, I wanted to read writing that explores the many dimensions of change, and is transformative in its own right. This new collection offers, I believe, a further vision of what is central to the creative lives of women. Between a writer and her work, between her work and the world, lies the territory of reciprocity.

Janet Sternburg

THE
WRITER
ON
HER WORK

VOLUME

II

THE NEED TO SAY IT

PATRICIA HAMPL

My Czech grandmother hated to see me with a book. She snatched it away if I sat still too long (dead to her), absorbed in my reading. "Bad for you," she would say, holding the loathsome thing behind her back, furious at my enchantment.

She kept her distance from the printed word of English, but she lavished attention on her lodge newspaper which came once a month, written in the quaint nineteenth-century Czech she and her generation had brought to America before the turn of the century. Like wedding cake saved from the feast, this language, over the years, had become a fossil, still recognizable but no longer something to be put in the mouth.

Did she read English? I'm not sure. I do know that she couldn't—or didn't—write it. That's where I came in.

My first commissioned work was to write letters for her. "You write for me, honey?" she would say, holding out a ballpoint she had been given at a grocery store promotion, clicking it like a castanet. My fee was cookies and milk, payable before, during, and after completion of the project.

I settled down at her kitchen table while she rooted around the drawer where she kept coupons and playing cards and bank calendars. Eventually she located a piece of stationery and a mismatched envelope. She laid the small, pastel sheet before me, smoothing it out; a floral motif was clotted across the top of the page and bled down one side. The paper was so insubstantial even ballpoint ink seeped through to the other side. "That's okay," she would say. "We only need one side."

True. In life she was a gifted gossip, unfurling an extended riff of chatter from a bare motif of rumor. But her writing style displayed a brevity that made Hemingway's prose look like nattering garrulity. She dictated her letters as if she were paying by the word.

"Dear Sister," she began, followed by a little time-buying cough and throat-clearing. "We are all well here." Pause. "And hope you are well too." Longer pause, the steamy broth of inspiration heating up on her side of the table. Then, in a lurch, "Winter is hard so I don't get out much."

This was followed instantly by an unconquerable fit of envy: "Not like you in California." Then she came to a complete halt, perhaps demoralized by this evidence that you can't put much on paper before you betray your secret self, try as you will to keep things civil.

She sat, she brooded, she stared out the window. She was locked in the perverse reticence of composition. She gazed at me, but I understood she did not see me. She was looking for her next thought. "Read what I wrote," she would finally say, having lost not only what she was looking for but what she already had pinned down. I went over the little trail of sentences that led to her dead end.

More silence, then a sigh. She gave up the ghost. "Put 'God bless you,' " she said. She reached across to see the lean rectangle of words on the paper. "Now leave some space," she said, "and put 'Love.' " I handed over the paper for her to sign.

She always asked if her signature looked nice. She wrote her one word—Teresa—with a flourish. For her, writing was painting, a visual art, not declarative but sensuous.

She sent her lean documents regularly to her only remaining sister who lived in Los Angeles, a place she had not visited. They had last seen each other as children in their village in Bohemia. But she never mentioned that or anything from that world. There was no taint of reminiscence in her prose.

Even at ten I was appalled by the minimalism of these letters. They enraged me. "Is that all you have to say?" I would ask her, a nasty edge to my voice.

It wasn't long before I began padding the text. Without telling her, I added an anecdote my father had told at dinner the night before, or I conducted this unknown reader through the heavy plot of my brother's attempt to make first string on the St. Thomas hockey team. I allowed myself a descriptive aria on the beauty of Minnesota winters (for the benefit of my California reader who might need some background material on the subject of ice hockey). A little of this, a little of that—there was always something I could toss into my grandmother's meager soup to thicken it up.

Of course the protagonist of the hockey tale was not "my brother." He was "my grandson." I departed from my own life without a regret and breezily inhabited my grandmother's.

I complained about my hip joint, I bemoaned the rising cost of hamburger, I even touched on the loneliness of old age, and hinted at the inattention of my son's wife (that is, my own mother, who was next door, oblivious to treachery).

In time, my grandmother gave in to the inevitable. Without ever discussing it, we understood that when she came looking for me, clicking her ballpoint, I was to write the letter, and her job was to keep the cookies coming. I abandoned her skimpy floral stationery, which badly cramped my style, and thumped down on the table a stack of ruled 8 ½ × 11.

"Just say something interesting," she would say. And I was off to the races.

I took over her life in prose. Somewhere along the line, though, she decided to take full possession of her sign-off. She asked me to show her how to write "Love" so she could add it to "Teresa" in her own hand. She practiced the new word many times on scratch paper before she allowed herself to commit it to the bottom of a letter.

But when she finally took the leap, I realized I had forgotten to tell her about the comma. On a single slanting line she had written: *Love Teresa.* The words didn't look like a closure, but a command.

Write about what you know. This instruction from grade school was the first bit of writing advice I was ever given. Terrific—that was just what I wanted to do. But privately, in a recess of my personality I could not gain access to by wish or by will, I was afraid this advice was a lie, concocted and disseminated nationwide by English teachers. The real, the secret, commandment was *Write about what matters.*

But they couldn't tell you that, I sensed, because nothing someone like me had experienced in the environs of St. Luke's grade school in St. Paul, Minnesota, mattered to anybody, and such a commandment would bring the whole creaking apparatus of assignments and spelling tests crashing down. I was never able to convince myself that anyone wanted to know what I had done on my summer vacation. They were just counting on my being vain enough to be flattered into telling. And they were right. But I resented it; I resented having nothing—really—to write about.

Maybe I wouldn't have fretted over the standard composition advice if I had valued my life in a simple way. Or rather, if I had valued the life around me. But literary types are born snobs, yearning for the social register of significance. And I was a literary kid from the get-go, falling into fairy tales and, later, enormous nineteenth-century novels as if into vats of imported heavy cream where I was perfectly content to drown.

I felt, I *believed,* my own life (and anything that touched it) was just so much still water. You could drown there too, but to no purpose, anonymous as a gasp, flailing around without experiencing the luscious sinking that made life worthwhile—which was literature. I wrote about princesses and angels. I filled in the silences left in familiar Bible stories, making up a travelogue about the flight into Egypt, fleshing out the domestic arrangements of Martha and Mary with a little dialogue: "Don't you expect me to do those dishes, Martha," huffed Mary. "The Lord's on my side."

Later, I wrote about lesbians (though I wasn't one) and a demented arsonist (though I was afraid to use my own fireplace at home). The beat went on: I was writing about things that mattered.

Later still, inevitably, I gave up, and wrote about my own life after all, first in poems, and then in a memoir whose main figure was my Czech grandmother. She who commanded love.

What bedevils me about this brief history of my literary attempts is that I ended up writing memoir (even the poems were routinely autobiographical), when that was the last thing I wanted to do. Wasn't it?

And as a subplot to this conundrum, how was it that I rattled on with stories and descriptions of "what I knew" in those letters I wrote for my grandmother in her kitchen, and yet it never dawned on me that this was *writing,* that this was *it.*

Put another way: how did I come to believe that *what I knew* was also *what mattered*? And, more to the point for the future, *is* it what matters?

Maybe being oneself is always an acquired taste. For a writer it's a big deal to bow—or kneel or get knocked down—to the fact that you are going to write your own books and not somebody else's.

Not even those books of the somebody else you thought it was your express business to spruce yourself up to be.

The recognition of one's genuine material seems to involve a fall from the phony grace of good intentions and elevated expectations. (I speak from experience, as memoirists are supposed to.)

A hush comes over the writing, an emotion akin to awe: so, something just beyond my own intelligence seemed to whisper when I began writing about my grandmother's garden which I couldn't imagine anyone caring about, it isn't a matter of whether you *can* go home again. You just do. Language, that most ghostly kind of travel, hands out the tickets. It never occurred to me, once given my ticket, to refuse it.

Yet, it wasn't the ticket I wanted. I didn't want to go home, I wanted to go—elsewhere. I wanted to write novels. Fat ones. Later, thinner ones—having moved from George Eliot to Virginia Woolf in my reading. But novels. About love and betrayal among grown-up modern men and women who should have behaved better (I thought). An important subject (I believed). A subject not given its due by men writers (I attested).

Instead, I've written memoir. And, so far, precious little love and betrayal of the sort I aspired to. Would that I could say that it's because I never experienced any betrayal along the way to or from love. But the equation between life and art hasn't proved to be so simple.

Still, I begin to see the elegance of a mathematical law in this confusion of impulse and execution, of intention and finished product: the material I was determined to elude has claimed me, while the subjects I wished to enlist in my liberation have spurned me.

Shame seems to be an essential catalyst in the business. Item: when I started college at the University in Minneapolis, I lost no time dumping the Catholic world my family had so carefully given me in St. Paul. In fact, that's why I went there: I understood many people had succeeded in losing their religion at the University. I didn't miss a beat turning down a scholarship at a Catholic college where I had been assured I would get more "individual attention." Who wanted individual attention? I wanted to be left alone to lose my soul.

For years, decades even, I considered it one solid accomplishment that I had escaped the nuns. Result: I have spent the better part of five years writing a memoir about growing up Catholic, a book which has taken me for extended stays at several monasteries and Catholic shrines in Europe and America. The central character of the book: a contemplative nun, the very figure I was determined to dodge.

Item: I was ashamed (though I didn't know it, couldn't have called it shame) that my Czech grandmother couldn't write English, that she was who she was at all. An immigrant is a quaint antecedent at a distance; mine was too close for the comfort of my literary ambition. The shame was real, disloyal, mean. Result: she came and got me, and became the heroine of my first memoir. She wrote it first: *Love Teresa*. And I did, finally.

Subject matter is only half the story. It may be possible to trace the lines leading to and from a writer's life and art in an attempt to reveal why someone writes about this and not about that. But form is a tougher nut: why a memoir, why not a novel?

I still puzzle over the reason I'm compelled to write books that deny me the pleasure of changing point of view, for instance. And admiring the straight spine of plot that gives the novel its grand carriage, why do I consort with a flabby genre with the habit of dithering aimlessly, fingering its pressed flowers from the recumbent swoon of reminiscence?

The memoir comes in for a lot of heat. It is accused of being a notorious bore, of betraying the beady mind of a grudge-bearer. Even the name—*memoir*—sounds lightweight, a designer genre with too much cheesy pastel between the lines. Invoking memoir is even a standard way of dismissing a bad novel: it's merely autobiographical.

For a while, I took refuge in the belief that at least memoir had the decency to make a fair contract with the reader. The prose promised no more and no less than it paid out: my mother, my father, my childhood, my perception of it all. No fancy overreaching omniscient narrators here. I grabbed the notion of honesty and hung on.

Then, a couple of years ago, a friend (a novelist, wouldn't you know it) ruined things. She had just read aloud from a novel she was working on. The reading was a hit, and everyone, including me, crowded around to praise her. The car ride to the family cabin, which opened the book, was especially strong; I could smell the pine needles, I told her. "Oh good," she said, a little shy, "that was our drive every year when I was a girl."

"Did you ever think of writing it as a memoir?" I said. It was an idle question, but it caught her off-guard.

"Oh no, I wouldn't write it as a memoir," she said, obviously repelled. "I want to tell the truth."

She looked embarrassed for an instant. It was purely social embarrassment, though; she is a courteous woman, and she was startled by her unvarnished candor in the face of the memoirist before her. She quickly recovered her novelist self, and looked right at me, her keen dark eyes holding their judgment: she wanted to tell the truth of her life—and memoir, she saw, doesn't encourage the truth.

My friend was not troubled by memory's habit of embracing the imagination. Long before, she had put her faith in the revelation of detail, not the accumulation of fact. Neither one of us was looking for a way to make literature a spreadsheet. The truth she felt memoir denied her was not the public truth of history or scholarship or journalism.

She mistrusted memoir because it would not allow her to speak her soul's truth. Paradoxically, memoir allowed less intimacy than fiction. Writing directly from her life did not provide fiction's free-dom to tell the truth derived from family secrets, from intensely personal events, from the burnt but still blooming core of the self. Memoir was left to explore the trivial—or to falsify the real. Or perhaps, its lowest sin: to make a mean little case against the past (a.k.a., mother and father).

I brooded on all that. I brood still.

Yet I wrote—I write—memoir. I had come to accept the inevita-ble tango of memory and imagination. I even looked forward to their inescapable encounter. It became one of the sharper pleasures of writing memoir: how uncanny to go back in memory to a house from which time has stolen all the furniture, and to find the one remembered chair, and write it so large, so deep, that it furnishes the entire vacant room. The past comes streaming back on words, and delivers the goods it had absconded with.

For all of that deep pleasure of retrieval, memoir is not about the past. As I understand it, memoir is not a matter of nostalgia. Its double root is in despair and protest (which, at first, seem no more kissing cousins than memory and imagination).

The despair comes from the recognition, impersonal but experi-enced as intensely intimate, that all things die. *Zip,* they're gone. Not only individual, ordinary lives (all of them, of course, all of *us*), but whole civilizations, rafts of accomplishments, gestures, mo-ments. Even the proper rage and horror at gigantic evil get eroded over time into conventional pieties. Nothing lasts, not even the solemn oath to remember.

The mind never gets over this betrayal of experience. In its dis-may, memory allies itself with the larger political and social sensibil-ity around it, the consciousness that makes people A People, a na-tion. This is the consciousness that causes the oppressed to take final refuge in culture, the consciousness that makes them willing to die—and kill—for a culture.

Out of the dread of ruin and disintegration emerges a protest which becomes history when it is written from the choral voice of a nation, and memoir when it is written from a personal voice. The dry twigs left of a vanished life, whatever its fullness once was, are rubbed together until they catch fire. Until they make something. Until they make a story.

Looked at this way, the truth memoir has to offer is not neatly opposite from fiction's truth. The methods and habits of memoir are different, and it is perhaps a more perverse genre than the novel: it *seems* to be about an individual self, but it is revealed as a minion of memory which belongs not only to the personal world, but to the public realm. As such, the greatest memoirs tend to be allergic to mere confession and mistrustful of revenge, though these are two of the genre's natural impulses. At least, I've felt these impulses, but I've never been able to make them stick on the page.

This refusal of memoir to display successfully raw confession or revenge is not, I'm sure, evidence of its inability to sustain personal truth. In fact, I like the mongrel nature of the genre that combines traits of fiction and of the essay, and lets just about anybody into the club.

I'm content to sit on the same bench with aging movie stars, with wistful sons who seem to know they'll never amount to much even though they've kicked their cocaine habit, with abused daughters trying to get back at famous fathers.

The memoir is not just a rest home for sensitive souls. Poets purveying acute angles of vision are there next to successful plaintiffs in palimony suits, and people whose fate has drawn them to Patagonia or away from Romania.

It's a quirk of the memoir that its narrator can never be its hero. Once again, it seems that memoir prefers the cooler, more neutral, term. The narrator is the protagonist—not the hero.

I'm used to being a protagonist by now, though that was not my original intention. No doubt, I'd write a very unconvincing heroine. I wonder if I'd even know how.

• • •

Writing about why you write is a funny business, like scratching what doesn't itch. Impulses are mysterious, and explaining them must be done with mirrors, like certain cunning sleight-of-hand routines. All the while I've been trying to grasp the reason I have written what I have in the manner I have, I've been working those mirrors for all they're worth.

Off to the side the whole time, in my lateral sight, has been a single snapshot, entirely accurate, I promise you, which I'm convinced possesses the complete explanation. How like a memoirist to believe a solo image, fluttering in the dark, is the rare butterfly that will, at last, complete the collection.

But I am a memoirist, so I'm off with my net: I'm in the sixth grade (blue serge uniform jumper, white blouse with Peter Pan collar). I'm still sitting in the second-to-last desk, in the row next to the windows. In a few months I will be moved forward, seat by seat, at my own troubled request until it is finally discerned that I need glasses.

But right now, I am still in that blessed outer region far from the blackboard and Sister's desk, still in the blur of undiagnosed myopia. And Mike Maloney, who doesn't love me (he *likes* me, he has said, making that distinction for me for the first time), sits behind me. We're pals. He is whispering something funny at the back of my head. That's gone forever.

Then Sister asks a question. I'd give a lot to know now what that question was. It's gone forever too, and I'm having a much harder time letting it go. Because I know the answer to this question. It's a really tough question and I just know nobody else in that class has the answer.

I've heard people talk about their hearts being in their throats, but I feel this extraordinary sensation—my *mind* or my brain or whatever is *me* is in my throat. I'm throbbing with the answer to that question, and my arm shoots up. It's waving crazily. I look like a drowning person grasping for help. But really I'm a bird, mighty with song. Sister has to call on me, I'll die if I can't crow out the answer. I reach to her, way from the back, my mad hand jumping.

She scans the room, *doesn't see me,* and turns to the board with her chalk. And provides the answer herself, just doles it out like medicine we all should take. And goes on with the lesson.

The throbbing in my throat actually hurts. My soul thuds inside me. Tears squint in my eyes from the raw denial I've been dealt. I'm aware, somewhere, that this whole thing is odd. But the main thing is, it's real. And I've got the answer and I've still got the wild need to say it.

I look out the window. We're on the third floor, and I see, below on the far playground, the other sixth-grade class at recess. I think I can make out Tommy Schwartz in his faded cords and plaid shirt and Sheila Phalen, wearing exactly what I am wearing. She is my best friend, we walk to school together; he is a basketball star, I adore him. Sheila alone knows this.

What are they doing together? I'll never know. But his head is bent slightly toward her. A new kind of misery enters me.

They're far away, I can barely make them out. Maybe it's not Tommy after all. But I've already pasted dreamy smiles on their faces. I squint, but that only blurs things. I have no desire to turn and talk to Mike Maloney who is right there behind me, and who likes me.

No. I want to communicate with those little indistinct figures way off there, who may or may not be Tommy and Sheila, who may or may not be pressing the first Valentine of love and betrayal into my palm, who may not even care that I have the answer. But I can't get rid of the ache in my throat which I know is my brain. I'll burst if I can't give my answer, that's all I know for sure.

A
FOUR-HUNDRED-YEAR-OLD
WOMAN

BHARATI MUKHERJEE

I was born into a class that did not live in its native language. I was born into a city that feared its future, and trained me for emigration. I attended a school run by Irish nuns, who regarded our walled-off school compound in Calcutta as a corner (forever green and tropical) of England. My "country"—called in Bengali *desh,* and suggesting more a homeland than a nation of which one is a citizen—I have never seen. It is the ancestral home of my father and is now in Bangladesh. Nevertheless, I speak his dialect of Bengali, and think of myself as "belonging" to Faridpur, the tiny green-gold village that was his birthplace. I was born into a religion that placed me, a Brahmin, at the top of its hierarchy while condemning me, as a woman, to a role of subservience. The larger political entity to which I gave my first allegiance—India—was not even a sovereign nation when I was born.

My horoscope, cast by a neighborhood astrologer when I was a week-old infant, predicted that I would be a writer, that I would win some prizes, that I would cross "the black waters" of oceans and make my home among aliens. Brought up in a culture that places its faith in horoscopes, it never occurred to me to doubt it. The astrologer meant to offer me a melancholy future; to be destined to leave India was to be banished from the sources of true culture. The nuns at school, on the other hand, insinuated that India had long outlived its glories, and that if we wanted to be educated, modern women and make something of our lives, we'd better hit the trail westward. All my girlhood, I straddled the seesaw of contradictions. *Bilayat,* meaning the scary, unknown "abroad," was both boom time and desperate loss.

I have found my way to the United States after many transit stops. The unglimpsed phantom Faridpur and the all too real Manhattan have merged as "desh." I am an American. I am an American writer, in the American mainstream, trying to extend it. This is a vitally important statement for me—I am not an Indian writer, not an exile, not an expatriate. I am an immigrant; my investment is in the American reality, not the Indian. I look on ghettoization— whether as a Bengali in India or as a hyphenated Indo-American in North America—as a temptation to be surmounted.

It took me ten painful years, from the early seventies to the early eighties, to overthrow the smothering tyranny of nostalgia. The remaining struggle for me is to make the American readership, meaning the editorial and publishing industries as well, acknowledge the same fact. (As the reception of such films as *Gandhi* and *A Passage to India* as well as *The Far Pavillions* and *The Jewel in the Crown* shows, nostalgia is a two-way street. Americans can feel nostalgic for a world they never knew.) The foreign-born, the exotically raised Third World immigrant with non-Western religions and non-European languages and appearance, can be as American as any steerage passenger from Ireland, Italy, or the Russian Pale. As I have written in another context (a review article in *The Nation* on books by Studs Terkel and Al Santoli), we are probably only a few years away from a Korean *What Makes Choon-li Run?* or a Hmong

Call It Sleep. In other words, my literary agenda begins by acknowledging that America has transformed *me*. It does not end until I show how I (and the hundreds of thousands like me) have transformed America.

The agenda is simply stated, but in the long run revolutionary. Make the familiar exotic; the exotic familiar.

I have had to create an audience. I cannot rely on shorthand references to my community, my religion, my class, my region, or my old school tie. I've had to sensitize editors as well as readers to the richness of the lives I'm writing about. The most moving form of praise I receive from readers can be summed up in three words: *I never knew.* Meaning, I see these people (call them Indians, Filipinos, Koreans, Chinese) around me all the time and I never knew they had an inner life. I never knew they schemed and cheated, suffered, felt so strongly, cared so passionately. When even the forms of praise are so rudimentary, the writer knows she has an inexhaustible fictional population to enumerate. Perhaps even a mission, to appropriate a good colonial word.

I have been blessed with an enormity of material. I can be Chekhovian and Tolstoyan—with melancholy and philosophical perspectives on the breaking of hearts as well as the fall of civilizations—and I can be a brash and raucous homesteader, Huck Finn and Woman Warrior, on the unclaimed plains of American literature. My material, reduced to jacket-flap copy, is the rapid and dramatic transformation of the United States since the early 1970s. Within that perceived perimeter, however, I hope to wring surprises.

Yet (I am a writer much given to "yet") my imaginative home is also in the tales told by my mother and grandmother, the world of the Hindu epics. For all the hope and energy I have placed in the process of immigration and accommodation—I'm a person who couldn't ride a public bus when she first arrived, and now I'm someone who watches tractor pulls on obscure cable channels—there are parts of me that remain Indian, parts that slide against the masks of newer selves. The form that my stories and novels take inevitably reflects the resources of Indian mythology—shape-changing, miracles, godly perspectives. My characters can, I hope, transcend the straitjacket of simple psychologizing. The people I write about are culturally and politically several hundred years old: consider the history they have witnessed (colonialism, technology, education, liberation, civil war, uprooting). They have shed old identities, taken on new ones, and learned to hide the scars. They may sell you newspapers, or clean your offices at night.

Writers (especially American writers, weaned on the luxury of affluence and freedom) often disavow the notion of a "literary duty" or "political consciousness," citing the all-too-frequent examples of writers ruined by their shrill commitments. Glibness abounds on both sides of the argument, but finally I have to side with my "Third World" compatriots: I do have a duty, beyond telling a good story or drawing a convincing character. My duty is to give voice to continents, but also to redefine the nature of *American* and what makes an American. In the process, work like mine and dozens like it will open up the canon of American literature.

It has not been an easy transition, from graduate student to citizen, from natural-born expatriate to the hurly-burly of immigration. My husband (Clark Blaise) and I spent fifteen years in his *desh* of Canada, and Canada was a country that discouraged the very process of assimilation. Eventually, it also discouraged the very presence of "Pakis" in its midst, and in 1980, a low point in our lives, we left, gave up our tenured, full-professor lives for the free-lancing life in the United States.

We were living in Iowa City in 1983 when Emory University called me to be writer-in-residence for the winter semester. My name, apparently, had been suggested to them by an old friend. I hadn't published a book in six years (two earlier novels, *The Tiger's Daughter* and *Wife,* as well as our joint nonfiction study, *Days and*

Nights in Calcutta, were out of print) but somehow Emory didn't hold it against me.

Atlanta turned out to be the luckiest writing break of my life. For one of those mysterious reasons, stories that had been gathering in me suddenly exploded. I wrote nearly all the stories in *Darkness* (Penguin, 1985) in those three months. I finally had a glimpse of my true material, and that is immigration. In other words, transformation—not preservation. I saw myself and my own experience refracted through a dozen separate lives. Clark, who remained in Iowa City until our younger son finished high school, sent me newspaper accounts, and I turned them into stories. Indian friends in Atlanta took me to dinners and table gossip became stories. Suddenly, I had begun appropriating the American language. My stories were about the hurly-burly of the unsettled magma between two worlds.

Eventually—inevitably—we made our way to New York. My next batch of stories (*The Middleman and Other Stories,* Grove, 1988) appropriate the American language in ways that are personally most satisfying to me (one Chicago reviewer likened it to Nabokov's *Lolita*), and my characters are now as likely to be American as immigrant, and Chinese, Filipino, or Middle Eastern as much as Indian. That book has enjoyed widespread support both critically and commercially, and empowered me to write a new novel, *Jasmine,* and to contract for a major work, historical in nature, that nevertheless incorporates a much earlier version of my basic theme, due for completion in the next three years. *Days and Nights in Calcutta* is being made into a feature film.

My theme is the making of new Americans. Wherever I travel in the (very) Old World, I find "Americans" in the making, whether or not they ever make it to these shores. I see them as dreamers and conquerors, not afraid of transforming themselves, not afraid of abandoning some of their principles along the way. In *Jasmine,* my "American" is born in a Punjabi village, marries at fourteen, and is widowed at sixteen. Nevertheless, she is an American and will enter the book as an Iowa banker's wife.

Ancestral habits of mind can be constricting; they also confer one's individuality. I know I can appropriate the American language, but I can never be a minimalist. I have too many stories to tell. I am aware of myself as a four-hundred-year-old woman, born in the captivity of a colonial, pre-industrial oral culture and living now as a contemporary New Yorker.

My image of artistic structure and artistic excellence is the Moghul miniature painting with its crazy foreshortening of vanishing point, its insistence that everything happens simultaneously, bound only by shape and color. In the miniature paintings of India, there are a dozen separate foci, the most complicated stories can be rendered on a grain of rice, the corners are as elaborated as the centers. There is a sense of the interpenetration of all things. In the Moghul miniature of my life, there would be women investigating their bodies with mirrors, but they would be doing it on a distant balcony under fans wielded by bored serving girls; there would be a small girl listening to a bent old woman; there would be a white man eating popcorn and watching a baseball game; there would be cocktail parties and cornfields and a village set among rice paddies and skyscrapers. In a sense, I wrote that story, "Courtly Vision," at the end of *Darkness*. And in a dozen other ways I'm writing it today, and I will be writing, in the Moghul style, till I get it right.

A SLEEVE OF RAIN

HARRIET DOERR

Sometimes in Mexico summer rain can be seen falling, all at one time, on isolated patches of the landscape. This is a selective rain, wetting the chapel in one village, the train station in another, a long empty stretch of highway in another. When these contained showers are distinguished against the mesas, people say, "It is raining in sleeves." A sleeve for Jesús María, a sleeve for Guadalupe de Atlas, a sleeve for every village and farm, if there is any sort of order at all under the skies.

Lately my memory, like those storms in Mexico, has begun to rain on me in sleeves. Today, writing at my desk on a March afternoon in California, I am deluged, without warning, by the contents of such a sleeve. All the houses I've ever lived in are raining down on me.

Three of them, destined to be objects of lifelong passion, were places that I knew by touch. My childhood sleeping porch, for instance. Long and narrow, it had been built onto the exterior of our house as the number of children multiplied from one to eight. Three cots, set head to foot in single file, entirely filled the porch. At the far end slept my oldest sister, Liz, at her feet the next oldest, Margaret, and finally, third in line, came my bed with me in it and my hand against the redwood shingles.

Now, falling from memory's sleeve are three small girls with only a wire screen between them and wind, hail, new moons, and shooting stars. They breathe in the dark and cold, bound by blankets to hard mattresses, a chamber pot beneath each bed.

But why the hand on the shingled wall? Even now, seventy-five years later and possessing at last the long view, I cannot say whether I touched the wood to claim the house, establish a connection, or simply for the sake of the shingles themselves, to feel their texture, to smell forest. I can resurrect them at will. I touch and smell them now.

Below the sleeping porch lay a garden, the nighttime province of gophers, frogs, and an occasional skunk. But when Liz was seventeen and had a party, Margaret and I watched shadows cross the lawn and listened to stifled laughter, urgent whispers, and an occasional silence so intense we almost heard it.

"They're necking," said Margaret, and together, two unseen, uncensorious witnesses, we moved closer to the screen.

For a better view, we looked down from the banister at the top of the stairs onto the heads and shoulders of dancing couples. "Moonlight on the Ganges" played a trio of piano, saxophone, and drums. "It Had to Be You." Boys we knew, pretending adulthood in starched wing collars and black bow ties, gathered at the living-room door.

"Stags," said Margaret, and we gazed as, dancing in and out of the arms of these boys, drifted girls in pale chiffon with artificial flowers at the hip.

Margaret pointed to Allie Riggs and Babs Perth, two of Liz's friends observed through the wide threshold to be sitting on a sofa just inside.

"Wallflowers," said Margaret.

A few boys brought flasks and, at the height of the party, disappeared at intervals into the garden shrubbery.

Margaret said, "Bootleg," and we continued to peer down as dancing couples began to Charleston. The band played "Ain't She Sweet?"

And here today, on this spring afternoon, now might as well be then. The old songs are raining on me from the sleeve.

Come to me, my melancholy baby, I can't give you anything but love. You were meant for me, I cried for you. Thou swell, I'll get by, side by side. Someone to watch over me, from Monday on, always.

After Liz, the rest of us grew up and, one by one, had parties of our own. Eventually, all four daughters of the family married husbands in the room where they had danced.

The living room had a wide fireplace, a piano much practiced on, a wall of books, and a reproduction of the *Winged Victory of Samothrace* in front of a window at one end. I could come here after school, bring ginger ale and graham crackers, fold myself into a chair, and, undisturbed, read *Missing* by Mrs. Humphrey Ward, *Graustark,* or *Les Miserables* for hours among my crumbs.

Directly overhead was my mother's room. Here she slept in the bed where five of her children were born and where, when the youngest was one, my father died.

Down the hall in a nursery turned schoolroom was the scarred round table where, chronologically, we learned to read and write. Our teacher was Miss Harriet Hannah Hutchins, who traveled ten miles each way on the streetcar to fill our minds with words and numbers and how to find Vesuvius on a map.

Miss Hutchins's skirts swept the floor, failing to conceal a pronounced limp. She wore a garnet ring on her engagement finger, a gold watch on a chain, and in the sun a black straw hat secured to her head by jet pins. The limp, we found out, was the result of a fall from a horse when she was sixteen. The ring was not explained, but all of us assumed that she had once been engaged to a soldier or a sailor killed in a war.

From time to time we visited the Hutchins family, who lived among lemon trees in a white Victorian cottage with a front porch crowded with potted ferns and wicker chairs. In one of these, a rocker, sat Miss Hutchins's mother, an old woman so small-boned, thin-haired, and creased it seemed impossible that even the country air, even smelling as it did of lemon blossoms, could sustain her. Beside her, in a straight chair, sat Miss Frances, Miss Hutchins's younger sister, so gentle and obviously so good that we sensed that she too, if only by her virtue, was somehow soon to perish.

In a corral across the drive, in the flickering shade of a mulberry tree, rested Miss Hutchins's aging horse Alec, whom we fed lumps of sugar from flat palms. Then, under the gaze of old Mrs. Hutchins and Miss Frances, we picked handfuls of mulberry leaves to feed the silkworms about to spin themselves into cocoons on the schoolroom shelf.

Once Miss Hutchins invited me to visit her father's grave. We drove to the cemetery in a buggy behind Alec. I held snapdragons and larkspur and she held the reins. It was a peaceful afternoon. I remember the clop of Alec's hooves, the fragrant groves on each side of us, and the high yellow sun above.

Arrived at the cemetery, we observed a moment's silence, while we stood on the grass beside a grave.

"My father lived to be eighty-nine," Miss Hutchins said. "He fought for the Union."

Familiar images gathered. Eliza on the ice. Lincoln at Gettysburg. General Lee and Traveler.

Then we drove back to the cottage in the absolute center of the same extraordinary peace.

Besides the silkworms, a hummingbird's nest with an egg in it and a stuffed wren were on display in the schoolroom. We found the nest one spring and, six months later, the expired bird, feet up on a gravel path. Without wasting a second, Miss Hutchins had wrapped it in her handkerchief and carried it to the schoolroom table, where she gutted and repacked it before our astonished eyes.

But what was the stuffing? Sand, grain, dry bread, or simply cotton batting? Did she sew up the feathered breast with darning thread? I saw the bird dead on the path. I saw it stuffed, its beak closed, its claws uncurled, perched on the bookcase. I believe I witnessed the reincarnation. But no matter. All of it, what I saw and what I didn't, is now the blood and bone of memory.

In the schoolroom during World War I we knitted balls of wool into ragged squares to help the American soldiers. When there were enough of these, they were collected to be sewn into blankets. And what odd blankets these must have been, knitted and purled by half-grown hands out of skeins of favorite colors.

Once you could make a square without dropping stitches, you could go on to mufflers. One day a letter came from an American soldier in France, thanking me for a muffler. I kept the yellowing pages for fifty years, through various changes of address and turnings out of closets, until finally, once and for all, it disappeared.

Miss Hutchins's era ended and we grew out of braces and into poetry. Often without warning Margaret, in her middy blouse and serge skirt, would fling open my door as I did homework and cry, "I have a rendezvous with death at some disputed barricade," or "If I should die, think only this of me . . ."

She knew all the repetitive poems by heart: "Boots, boots, boots, boots," "The highwayman came riding, riding, riding," and "Go down to Kew in lilac time, in lilac time, in lilac time."

On the evening of the day she bobbed her hair, she struck my door open and called out, "What lips my lips have kissed, and where, and why, I have forgotten," going on with scarcely a pause to "Last night, ah, yesternight, betwixt her lips and mine there fell thy shadow, Cynara, and the night was thine." And we were both impaled on the words.

Outside the room where these performances took place stretched the sleeping porch. From where I sat, dipping my pen into ink, I had only to take two steps and reach through a window to touch the redwood shingles, feel their rough grain.

Beyond the porch and the lawn, entirely separated from care and cultivation by an evergreen hedge, sloped a wild hillside of oaks, eucalyptus, weeds, and Matilija poppies, whose crushed tissue-paper petals unfolded every June into white flowers as big as a child's face.

Halfway down this hill an ancient acacia, which still produced a few yellow clusters in the spring, supported a tree house, consisting of two platforms of pine boards. Its lack of a roof and walls failed to diminish our pleasure in it. Here we played and quarreled and took up candy bars to eat.

Sometimes I had the tree house to myself. Then I would sit cross-legged on the top floor and watch the afternoon turn into night. I realize now that these were my only chances, alone in the tree house, to ache. Without interruptions or observers, to ache for the world, and for me in it.

I had left the house where I was born and had a husband and child when Miss Hutchins was brought down by cancer. I took some late roses and a few spikes of lavender to the hospital and she tried to notice them. She was too tired to speak. It was only when I stood up to go that Miss Hutchins said, in a voice I hardly knew, "The pain is unendurable. I cannot stand the pain." Then added, "I have talked to the doctor." She died eleven days, or 264 hours, later.

Now all the other houses are raining from the sleeve.

First is an old California adobe my husband and I and our small children lived in for five years. Built in 1816 as a grist mill for a Franciscan mission, it had already been named a historic monument when we moved in. Surviving age, earthquakes, and damage by occupants, the mill stood solid and pristine in a revised neighborhood. A nearby lake had long since been drained, the surrounding fields and groves turned suburb. But the old building, its original white walls weathered to faded gold, continued to exist intact on its acre, inside its high outer wall, immune to change, out of context and out of time.

"How is it to come in from the street and step through the gate in your wall?" people asked us.

And we said, "Magic."

For it was all enchanted. The high beams tied with leather thongs, the windows set in walls four feet thick, the whitewashed interior, the border that took the place of baseboards, painted with vegetable colors in an Indian design.

The old mill absorbed anachronisms. No matter that my first typewriter occupied a table in a bedroom or that a model airplane hung from a sycamore tree. No difference the diapers drying in front of the living room fire or the tricycle in the patio. If Junípero Serra himself had walked in, he would only have had to touch the walls to know that he was home.

The garden claimed a few witnesses from the past, a bent black walnut tree, a gnarled olive, and a Castilian rose. Filling up the space around them, orange trees flowered and bore fruit, the red blossoms of a hedge turned into a hundred pomegranates in the fall, and a dozen plants that looked like giant thistles produced long-stemmed artichokes.

On weekend mornings in the old mill, we were often roused from sleep by the arrival outside of unexpected visitors. Some of them only came to look and, if the light was right, take pictures. Others came to work. From our bedroom my husband and I, still in nightgown and pajamas, would gaze down on painters, settled on

stools before their easels, or on persons carrying maps who scientifi-
cally paced the ground between the walls. These were treasure hunt-
ers, searching for Spanish gold.

"The Franciscan fathers are known to have buried it here," they
told us, but the distances on the maps never corresponded to the
dimensions of the garden.

Once an elderly man made himself at home with a divining rod
and for two April days moved slowly between tree and path, grape-
vine and agave.

"It's got to be here somewhere," he said.

"Is it in doubloons?" we asked, and he nodded.

He left empty-handed, but we agreed with him. It had to be here
somewhere.

In the bedroom that used to be a granary I composed a number of
poems that rhymed, usually in quatrains, and submitted them to
magazines. These, not surprisingly and without exception, failed.
Fifty years later I still have the printed rejections. Unlike the hand-
written note from the soldier of World War I, they were never lost.

It was from this house, when I was twenty-five, that I first traveled into the interior of Mexico. Not just to a border town, as
previously, but to the heart of the country, Mexico City, three days
and nights by train behind a steam locomotive.

We stayed in a post-colonial house a block from the Paseo de la
Reforma, between the *glorietas* of the Diana and the Angel. In the
center of one, the goddess of the hunt, circled by traffic, lifted her
bow and arrow over thirty mongrels lapping at the basin below. In
the second, from the top of a soaring column, a golden angel raised a
laurel wreath over buses, trucks, carts, and sidewalks crowded with
vendors, beggars, pedestrians, and petty thieves.

The house of our relatives was dark, high-ceilinged, and, except at
midday, cold. During a week's visit, I was never allowed to enter the
kitchen, where a barefoot, loose-braided family retainer named
Maria de Jesús kept a parrot on a perch above the casseroles, occa-

sionally encouraging it to fly. Old, gold-toothed, homesick for the distant place where she was born, she survived by recreating it among the alien pots and pans.

On this first trip to Mexico, I went to an Aztec pyramid, to the canals on whose banks flowers are grown, to the opera house which sinks lower a fraction of an inch each day, and to a nightclub. I see now that in this week I failed utterly to penetrate the surface of Mexico. But was it then that the spell fell on me?

I have lived most of fifty years in the California hillside house where I write today. But, in spite of its long history of Christmases and birthdays, measles and chicken pox, music lessons and menageries, I have little to say of it. As long as I continue to inhabit it, how am I to see it plain and clear? We are not through with each other, this house and I.

When we had lived here nine years, we rented its wistaria vine and windows with views to a safe tenant and moved to a house with a crimson door in Mexico City. This house backed into a hill and had adjacent structures on both sides, so that all its rooms faced front.

To enter, you opened a narrow red door next to a wide red one that closed the garage. Then you continued along a red passageway toward a glass aviary on an upper level. This bird cage served as the fourth and outside wall of the red dining room, which lay directly behind.

And now, out of memory's sleeve, falls a shower of birds. For in this cage lived crested cardinals, perching listlessly on defoliated twigs or pecking for seeds mixed with gravel on the aviary floor.

While we ate our egg, sandwich, or chop, in the blood-red dining room, we gazed at the matching birds. Sometimes one of us rose from the table and tapped on the glass to remind the cardinals that we, too, swam in this crimson sea.

At the end of the first week, we visited a specialist at the pet store.

"*Cardinales,*" he said, and fell silent. Then he said, "They are molting," and we said, "Yes."

"They have light," he said, and we said, "No," and explained that, although the aviary faced the street, a pepper tree had grown between it and the sun.

"*Caray!*" the man said, contracting "*Caramba,*" and sold us food supplements of vitamin D.

The next day we asked our landlady to remove the cardinals.

"They are better off in the aviary," she said. "Outside they would be pecked to death by other birds."

Was it one, or was it two cardinals that died of chronic deprivation during our year's tenancy? And did we replace them when we left, as we did a few glasses and a cup? But, by that time, the whole situation had changed. For as the cardinals declined above, field mice began to enter through a hole in the aviary floor and forage for fallen seed. Even rounder and tamer than the creations of Potter and Disney, the fattening mice somehow compensated for the daily worsening of the birds.

Our dinner guests, entranced, ate with eyes fixed on the glass cage. Like visitors to a zoo, they pondered the mice and the birds. They asked to be invited back.

The house with the red door had a flat roof where clothes were washed and hung to dry. On the roof, which was 7,500 feet above sea level, the air was like sea air, light and crisp. If not for the hill behind the house, we could have stood here, looked over the city, its parks, palaces, and slums, and beyond, over farms, fields, and Indian ruins, all the way to the volcanos, Popo and Ixti, the two lovers under the snow.

Years later we took possession of the second white adobe in our lives. This one was in central Mexico, a day's drive from the capital, at the edge of a village of little water and few trees, a place whose inhabitants burned and shivered according to the season within a circle of barren hills. But not barren at all, of course, if you count rocks and their formations. Almost as soon as we arrived, trucks started bringing loads of these rocks to our house, for a wall, for a border, for some steps. When the mason split them, they broke into halves of all shades of rose and green and sand. Some had blue streaks. Some were speckled with gold. Each was as individual as a piece of jade. You knew them best by touching them, by moving along the half-finished wall, your hand sliding from one rough surface to the next. Dry, hard, complex, indifferent, they were the fiber of our world.

"How old are they?" you might ask.

"Ay, quién sabe?" the mason said. "As old as all of it," and he would wave an arm from one horizon to the other, encompassing mountains, fields, cows, goats, a church dome, the hoist tower of an idle mine, geraniums in a pot, a lizard on a tile. He had no thought of millenniums of fire and ice, of convulsions at the planet's core. The mason only meant the rocks were as old as the day when the whole idea occurred to God.

The true sound of Mexico is not the braying of the burro or the baying of the coyote, nor is it the plaint of the beggar or the passion in a song. The true, infallible, recognizable sound is the pounding of the mason's chisel against stone.

Our early mornings in this place were all alike. We woke in our square, beam-ceilinged room first to sunrise, then, in this order, to cock crow, church bell, bird song, and the rhythmic chipping away of stone. We bathed and brushed our teeth to the sound of it, spoke and ate to it.

We met the mason on our first day in the village. Twenty-five years later, when I left for the last time, his son, a master of the same craft, stood in the driveway to see me off. He was one of a small crowd that had gathered. When the last things, my thermos and my sandwich, were in the car, I shook hands with each one, the watchman, his daughter and grandson, the cook, the carpenter, the electrician-mechanic turned majordomo, the boy who gardened, and the man who every spring borrowed our empty field to plant his corn.

When I looked back from the gate, they were all still there and I almost stopped to lean out and wave again.

But such a thing was impossible. They would have thought I had forgotten something and come after me to help.

I would have had to say, "Oh, no, I've left nothing behind," and thank them again. I would have said, "See for yourselves. It is all here," and, for the second time, left it all behind.

Eventually some Mexican stones found their way to my California garden. Geodes sometimes appear when ivy is cut back. A rock that was once the color of amethyst has taken a permanent place under an orange tree. Birds drink from a shell carved from *cantera,* the marble of Mexico.

"Do you want to keep these rocks?" asks the gardener, whose mother as a child fled a village not far from ours during the Revolution of 1910. He looks at half a dozen ore samples, some still showing copper, some still showing lead, scattered without purpose along a brick border.

And I say, "Yes. Keep them," knowing that as soon as his back is turned, I will take one up and immediately enter that other garden two thousand miles to the south. It is noon and hot. I can pick the first ripe fig. I can touch the first hard-fought-for rose.

From the desk where I write today, I face a window three-quarters full of sky. At my left hand is a chip of copper ore that shows azurite. For no other reasons than these, I see all at once that everything is possible. I have recovered my houses. Now I can bring back the rest, picnics and circuses, train rides and steamers, labels on trunks, and wreaths for the dead on front doors.

I have everything I need. A square of sky, a piece of stone, a page, a pen, and memory raining down on me in sleeves.

MY MOTHER, LITERATURE, AND A LIFE SPLIT NEATLY INTO TWO HALVES

KAYE GIBBONS

My Mother

It started with my mother, this writing urge. I do believe it started with her. She never surprised me with handsome leather-bound editions of anything. She never recited poetry to me as she brushed and braided my hair. She never even called out my spelling words. But nonetheless, I think it began with her.

She was a good country woman. She kept crocheted doilies pinned to the backs and arms of chairs. She could snap a live chicken's neck quick as a wink, and clean and dress the thing in time for supper. She was lighting the pilot light in the oven when they announced John F. Kennedy was dead, and she sat right down on the kitchen floor and cried. That was the first time I realized she thought of things besides hot breakfasts, sterile Mason jars, quilts, and the square of clay dirt we tried to farm. She never elaborated on her feelings. She just cried and held me around my knees when I walked over to her. That is my first memory of her.

One day I rode with my parents to haul a load of tobacco to market. I was still short enough to stand between them, and I remember feeling thrilled that Mama was driving the big truck. She must have been afraid my father would spill us and the tobacco out of the truck, so she took charge of getting the baby girl, one load of tobacco, and one loaded farmer to market on time. She looked small behind the wheel, and she had to slide down in the seat to mash the pedals. And even now when my gears stick I can see and hear my father laugh and swipe the liquor off his lips and say to my mother: If you can't find it, G R I N D I T !

Grinding it was her specialty. She forced the gears on the farm truck to click into place and we sold the tobacco that day. And on that day and days like that, I saw my mother make a stern face and pull needles through English smocking, spit on irons, and level the bangs on my Buster Brown.

Her name was Shine, which is exactly what she did through all the heat and poverty and the sad certainty that life would not be any other way. Her strength was a fine thing to see, to remember. If I had not known that strength, that pure perseverance, I could not have become a writer. I would have chosen something that takes far less courage.

I said I would have chosen something, but there was never really any choice. Writing was and is something I need to do just as my mother needed to get that crop to market. Any crop, be it tobacco or language, must be harvested and prepared when it is ripe, and I am learning to work with my imagination just as my mother understood the seasons on our farm, the bright green of tobacco in its prime, the right time for sowing, the best time for watering. She stayed busy with getting by and managing. She called that "going and doing." *I need to get the strawberries in the freezer before lunch so I can go and do this afternoon.* And she'd wear herself out going and doing.

I don't have any corn or tobacco or even strawberries, just two raggedy peach trees that may or may not bear fruit this year. But I do have words, and they'll come in their own time, in their own way. And I have the freedom to let my imagination go and do, made possible by a stable home, something she never had. And out of that imaginative roaming comes artistic creation, something else she never experienced, unless one views survival as an act of creation in and of itself.

Literature

Amidst all my mother's working and my father's Snopesian not going and not doing, I watched as much television as I could and read books when the networks' offerings did not suit me. After her death in 1970, I used television and then books to fill the remarkable void she had left. I'd stand in the living room and sing all the show tunes with vigor, doing the best I could with unfamiliar words and phrases, as with the *Green Acres* song: *I just adore the pink house fumes. . . . Keith Manhattan just gave me Park Avenue.* I'd think, Mighty generous of that Keith Manhattan.

Although I'd watch anything the networks put forth, I would not read just anything. I remember snubbing Nancy Drew, the Madeleine series, and similar stories for young girls. The characters, I thought, were silly and the writing had no snap to it, much too ordinary. I suppose hours of *Get Smart* had honed my tastes, groomed me for higher art.

In the fourth grade I remember bringing a collection of Edgar Allan Poe stories and poems home from the bookmobile. I probably selected the book because it was huge, full of etchings and rubrics, exotic and generally just my style. I'd scare myself stiff reading and having what I'll swear were out-of-the-body experiences inside those etchings. As soon as I'd recover I'd read more. "Annabel Lee" was perfect. I'd memorize five or six lines at a time so I could terrify myself even when I did not have access to the book. "The Tell-Tale Heart" and "The Gold Bug" became standards against which I measured everything I read, and when I found a biography of Poe, no doubt watered down for young readers, I became even more convinced that this wild, cursed genius was the greatest writer of all time. He held that rank until I read "Let me not to the marriage of true minds" in the poetry section of the World Book Encyclopedia.

That year my language arts teacher, who looked very much like Margaret Thatcher, asked the class to memorize and recite a poem of our choice. Mine was Shakespeare's Sonnet 116, and I surprised even myself with the passion of my performance. Thank goodness she didn't ask me to define "impediment" or explain "his bending sickle's compass come." That theatrical moment was only rivaled five years ago when an elegantly intoxicated friend sang Emily Dickinson's "Because I Could Not Stop for Death" to the tune of "The Yellow Rose of Texas." Now I do that every chance I get.

That early dramatic episode pretty well solidified my reputation as an odd child. But I didn't mind. In fact, I luxuriated in my peculiarity, or that's what I thought I was doing. Now I think I was overcompensating, straining to be heard and applauded. Perhaps writing is an attempt at mitigating that early frustration.

As strange as I felt, as strange as I was, my life's ambition was to be a lab technician. I visualized the test tubes, the litmus paper, the white jacket, and sensed the order and security of it all. That goal was no doubt a reaction to the chaos that swirled in my home after my mother's death. It took nearly five years for my life to realign itself, and when it did my ambition also altered. By the time I was sixteen I'd decided that the rapid accumulation of as much wealth as possible was far more important than laboratory science, so I chose the law as my life's work. And not only would I become wealthy, I'd also become famous for saving countless innocent men from unjust execution, arguing countless cases before the Supreme Court, and generally changing the world. However, somewhere between ages sixteen and nineteen I realized that most lawyers never meet even one man falsely accused of some heinous crime and that many of the more mundane legal tasks require about as much imagination as testing a streptococcus culture.

I was writing by then, but I didn't want to be a writer. I thought only famous writers earned enough money or respect to have any sort of job satisfaction. The only famous writer I'd ever come close to almost meeting was Jack Kerouac, who'd spent some time on the Langley farm, about three miles from my home. I never saw him, but Jackie Langley told me Kerouac was a strange bird, stayed drunk, talked crazy, brooded. Although I was also a strange bird, I didn't see any reason to grow up and cloister myself in some farm shack, freeze in the winter, sweat in the summer, fight flies, and eat cold collards for the sake of art or anything else. I'd already played that game. I've since decided that Kerouac's coming to our little community to suffer, get in touch with himself, find universal truths, whatever, was a little silly, if not insulting. As much as he was wanting in that place, I was wanting out. He might've been amused with a place that was yet to feel the trickle-down effects of such notions as civil rights, evolution, and women's liberation, but I was not. We were both strange birds, artistic in our own ways, but I wanted to fly that coop.

I read myself out of my community, my past, but still in college I didn't want to be a writer. I was writing more, but I considered writing and being a writer two different enterprises altogether, and I still do. By my sophomore year I'd lost all ability and desire to visualize my life outside of school. It was a haven. It always had been. I knew the rules there, and if I didn't succeed I knew it was due to my own refusal to play by those rules. My happiness there didn't depend on chance, such as the chance of my mother being sick on a holiday or the likely chance that my father would look out at a hailstorm and say he wished he'd remembered to mail that hail insurance premium. I decided that the best thing I could do for myself was to stay in school forever, to study and then teach literature and then go out Mr. Chips style.

I began to learn and know literature better than I wanted to know myself or any other person. English literary history was my particular obsession. It seemed to have an order, patterns, logically proceeding from Caedmon to Ted Hughes, and the entire system of language and thought fairly well amazed me.

Through high school and college I read everything I could as methodically and painstakingly as I could. And I feel pretty safe saying that I rarely read anything for pleasure, although I've derived what I would call pure ecstasy obsessing over lines from T. S. Eliot or Gerald Manley Hopkins, my little Oxford English Dictionary magnifying glass in hand, hellbent on getting at that one true meaning. Even as I spent bizarre amounts of time scrutinizing a poem I've said to myself, This is not normal, may be a little freakish, but I couldn't stop. I've read in *National Geographic* that certain pygmy tribes derive a similar thrill by carving into their persons with hot porcupine needles.

During this period I also ran through a rather bizarre assortment of friends, from squeaky clean fraternity boys to the most militant feminists. See, I knew I was a woman, but I didn't know what that meant, so I tried on faces as deliberately and as thoughtfully as I was conducting the literary part of my life. And still I had the memory of my mother, but nothing in her life seemed applicable to me then. I'd never thought of her as a woman, at least not the kind of woman who taught my Chaucer class or those who came up on Saturdays and took their sororitied daughters shopping for the Sigma Chi ball or took the floor at N.O.W. meetings and cursed and cried when the Equal Rights Amendment failed. My mother seemed then to have been somebody who was loved too little, worked too hard, and spun herself out with the working. So when I looked around me those first two years of college, the ways to live, the ways of being a woman seemed to stretch out as long as all the books I wanted to read. I wanted to find a way, very simply, to be.

So there I was at twenty-two, with absolutely no idea what to do with myself when the school bell rang. If I had not met and married my husband I have every reason to believe I'd still be wandering around a campus somewhere, growing more and more reluctant to acknowledge the line between art and reality.

A Life Split Neatly into Two Halves

My memory houses a collection of images, not ordered in the patterns I see and respect in literary history, not ordered in any form vaguely resembling a chronology. I have to work at telling when something happened and then what happened next. There seem to be so many gaps, and I know the gaps are there thanks to this incredible mind machine we possess that filters pain, protects us, that knows, as T. S. Eliot knew: *Humankind cannot bear very much reality.*

I've never been very good at making myself do anything or making myself stop doing anything. More than once I've attempted complete and lasting mind and body overhauls and ended up in worse shape than when I started, so when I married, birthed a baby, and generally looked after myself and two other people I astonished everyone who'd ever bemoaned my inability to get on in life, everyone who'd bemoaned my refusal to embrace anything but a book.

My life changed with the marriage and the birth, and the memory of my mother escorted me through the transition from a girl who loved literature better than her life to a woman who overcame her past and got at the business of living.

Having my first child made me feel part of the human race. I'd always believed my pain and little bursts of joy to be unique. But that feeling of separateness abates, it must, when one is in labor, crying then screaming then laughing, and then hearing some other woman doing the same. When Mary was born, my husband held her and welcomed her to the planet. I knew that greeting applied to me, too.

I spend as much time thinking about my family now as I used to spend absorbed in literature. I watch them. I'm learning them and their patterns, listening to my older daughter make her way around the English language, and that's no less than miraculous.

If I can be anything to my daughters, I wish to be a bridge from my mother to them. They'll never witness their mother wringing a chicken's neck, but they will hear about how it's done as soon as they're old enough to appreciate it. I want my mother's strength to pass through me to them. I'm not talking about that kind of tweedy pump-footed stamina that crunches knuckles on the way up the corporate ladder, nor do I mean the kind of placard-waving tough-ness that derides cheerleaders, belles of the ball, and nice girls who don't (or do). That behavior is picked up along the way.

I watched my mother open bills, stand up a little straighter, and place new notices on the stack of old ones we hadn't paid. I remem-ber thinking we were very popular to get all that mail. When I was old enough to read, I fumbled through the stack and felt frightened and rushed inside to know we were so past due on everything, that everything was threatened, just damned. I believe she held on to hope, then to the memory of one time having hope, and when trying to hang on to a memory of so long past seemed silly and useless, she gave up. I understand her better now, and I think by letting her memory help me I'm making my peace with her, with my own past. Any truce must come of understanding.

Since my first novel *Ellen Foster* was published I've read many articles about my own supposed Cinderella story: student shows thirty pages of a manuscript to her teacher who turns out to be a publisher and so forth and so on and they all live happily ever after. This often sounds more like an accusation than a celebration. No-body saw me paying the sort of price typically associated with getting a first novel published and noticed. I've never enjoyed the company of people who believe that by living a "writerly" life, complete with rejection notices papering the walls, the writing will follow. Dues payments are not self-conscious acts. I've never believed anyone can will the mind to create a thing of beauty. I like to think artistic creation starts in a more mysterious place, somewhere deep within, probably somewhere way far back in one's past.

So I did pay dues. I don't have a shoebox full of rejection notices, but I paid them. Like writers I love and who have kept me company through my life, I paid them when I was a child and was separate and apart, when I learned to see the place I was in as an observer and, as much as I hate to admit it, as one who was intrinsically wrapped up in the seasons on that farm, that heat and poverty, and that sad certainty that life would not be any other way.

My mother's death both freed me and marked me. When she died I was able to physically leave the place I'd been making little mind excursions from ever since I learned to read. If she were still living I would still be bound to my old home, and I know I would not have turned to literature and used it as I have.

So I believe that it is under the incredible burden of memory that I write, and I cannot trade my memory, as much as I've often wanted to do so. My past is what it is. All the memory will allow me or any other writer to do is order it through language.

I write about what I know best. And if death and sorrow and the inexplicable joy that comes from triumph over death and sorrow, if these themes are predominant in my work, past and future, it is because they dominate my memory. That joy and hope are recent finds for me, found in the faces of a good man and three babies. Someone once told me that writing is an act of faith. Another person told me that forgiving is also an act of faith. That's true. I think both heal, both are an art. What a fine thing it is to do both at once.

THE CARE-GIVERS

MAXINE KUMIN

August 1989

This summer I am serving *in loco parentis* to my six-and-a-half-year-old grandson, who crossed the Atlantic Ocean alone on the competent wings of Swiss Air to stay with us on the farm. The days are energetic, filled with horses and barn work, pea- and raspberry-picking, swims in the pond and romps with the dogs, and he is a cheerful and outgoing child. But after sunset as the dark comes on, his defenses drop. He grows homesick and teeters on the verge of tears. I read to him or he reads to me. We talk. I stay in the room with him until he is asleep. This ritual round of days sharpens for me my memories of the early fifties when I was housebound, dutiful, and diligent, baking cookies, making salt dough for small hands to pummel, reading aloud, pacifying and feeding three youngsters born between October of 1948 and June of 1953.

Thirty-six years ago! The women's movement had not yet acquired enough leaven to declare itself. The stewpot of discontent in which I simmered had no name, no authenticity, no support group. I had a master's degre in comparative literature, all undusted and unused. I worked part-time nights and weekends ghosting articles for various medical journals; my best client was a German psychiatrist afflicted with interminable sentences. Luckily, we were poor and the money I earned was significant, which gave my work some stature.

It is hard for me to particularize what I was feeling then. Whatever it was—depression, anomie, an inwardly raging discontent—was heavily encrusted with guilt. Why wasn't I happy? I was, after all, living exactly the life that had been programmed for me. We had come through World War II unscathed. We had married young, after a passionate courtship, we had mortgaged ourselves to the neckstem to escape from a succession of apartments, bought a house in a Boston suburb noted for its good public schools, and we were raising a family. I was fulfilling all the expectations of my generation, but it left me emotionally drained, flattened, even despairing. I was realistic enough not to expect ecstasy, but where was a sense of satisfaction? Where, shining in the distance, was there a goal?

From the dawning of literacy in my early childhood, I had written stories and poems, creatively misspelled. As a teenager I had contributed reams of fiction and verse to the school magazine. I had been editor of the school newspaper. At Radcliffe I continued to write in every available genre, and it was at Radcliffe that I got my comeuppance. A young instructor in an advanced composition class handed back a sheaf of exceedingly romantic poems with the advice that I "say it with flowers, but for God's sake don't write any poems about it." I was a seventeen-year-old freshman and this pronouncement from on high totally devastated me; I did not write another poem for eight years. Let me just say, parenthetically, that this incident taught me something essential. In all the years I have spent doing workshops and seminars at a variety of universities around the United States, I have tried hard not to trample on the fragile egos of young would-be writers. I don't think any professor of any stature—and my young instructor went on to become a famous novelist—can know where a student author is going. I have seen dozens of truly exciting, promising young poets and fictioneers drift off into other, more immediately compelling, lines of work. I have seen relatively inarticulate, groping young writers coalesce, converge, grow up—whatever the yeast is—and rise to astonishing heights. I see now that these successes and failures are beyond the control of the most dedicated teacher. John Ciardi used to say that the workshop teacher is merely "a hired sympathy." I tend to agree with him. Prosody and matters of style can be taught, but the well-springs of talents will bubble up on their own.

In my own case, having been warned away from the serious practice of poetry, I sought another outlet. It was the winter of 1952–53. I saw, advertised in *The Writer* magazine, a little text by Richard Armour called *Writing Light Verse.* I believe it cost $3.95; I sent away for it.

A secret plan was taking shape. I struck a bargain with myself. Pregnant for the third time, I vowed to have sold a poem before this baby was born or else to abandon forever the childhood goal of becoming a real writer.

On March 17, 1953, the *Christian Science Monitor* bought the following quatrain:

Factually Speaking

There never blows so red the rose,
So sound the round tomato
As March's catalogues disclose
And yearly I fall prey to.

Soon I was appearing in the *Monitor* quite regularly. I sold similar "filler" verses to the *Saturday Evening Post, Good Housekeeping,* the

New York Herald Tribune, the *Wall Street Journal,* and several other periodicals and journals. I developed a card file, using an old recipe box—how appropriately ironic that seems to me now!—and by the time Danny Kumin was born on June 13, 1953, I had established a thriving cottage industry.

It seemed essential to carry on this business without in any way neglecting housewifery and motherhood. I learned how to write in the interstices of daily life and I was aided in this complicity by the fact that a small poem is infinitely portable. Reaching for an apt rhyme, a clever ending, or a richly ambiguous title can take place while performing all the daily indigenous acts that keep a household fed and watered, loved and laundered. There was no question in my mind then—we are speaking of the early fifties, remember—which came first. I paid fealty to my chosen role as wife and mother. The Muse had to stumble along subsisting on crumbs of time, for to work outside the home in the middle-class canon of behavior was to neglect your family.

There was a man so poor / he fell in love with jail, goes an old saying. It never occurred to me then that I was the willing victim of sexism. In fact, I was faring far better than most of my contemporaries. I was married to a man who changed diapers, did dishes and laundry, believed in equal parenting, and hugely encouraged my writing dreams. The pressures to conform came from *me.* The stricture to write only humorous verses also came from within. For hadn't I been admonished not to get serious about deeply held feelings? All these years later, it occurs to me that laughter is a way of dealing with emotion. Wit is often a foil for pain; humor can mask hardship. Admittedly, light verse focuses on our common foibles. It pokes gentle fun, points out simple paradoxes. It is above all *safe,* obeying the maxim: Laugh and the world laughs with you. Nevertheless, learning how to shape a successful bit of filler verse teaches you something about metrics. Light verse relies mightily on rhyme, too, especially on unexpected but apt resonances. Then there is the matter of endings. A good piece of humorous verse turns on the latch of strong closure. The last lines had better rhyme well, make a sharp point, and announce the end of the poem with the definitive click of the door closing on its jamb.

It was a strange school in which to hone my skills. I was, then, too cowardly to undertake anything more taxing or authentic but I desperately wanted to write real poems. I haunted the Grolier, the one bookshop in Cambridge that specialized in poetry books. I read all of the post–World War II poets—Jarrell and Nemerov, Shapiro, Spender, Auden—especially Auden, whose magical tetrameter lines seemed to me to capture wit and feeling in one embrace. I vaguely knew I wanted to do something like that. I do not think I was aware, except very marginally, that there were virtually no women among these stalwarts. From time to time, I tiptoed in alone to poetry readings at the universities in and around Boston. Gradually, I began writing my own true poems in the dark. I did not know what exactly to make of these, for they were the very obverse of the cheerful, determinedly upbeat verses I sold to the *Saturday Evening Post* or to *Baby Talk.* Many of them were about the end of the world. They were woolly and thick with abstractions. I did not then understand that what I needed was "a hired sympathy." In 1957 I found one.

John Holmes, poet and professor of English at Tufts University, also conducted a poetry workshop at the Boston Center for Adult Education. Early in the winter of 1957 I made my way, rather shyly, into his classroom at the Center. Anne Sexton and I met in that group; we discovered, that first evening, that we had each driven into Boston alone from suburban Newton. Thus began our intense personal and professional friendship. It was to endure until her suicide in October of 1974.

Sexton and I each published a first book of poems as a result of that workshop experience, she in 1960 and I in 1961. It confirmed for me the value of workshops, at least of good workshops where passion and empathy mingle and a poet can try out a new poem on trained and thoughtful ears. For this is a lonely calling; I do not know a single poet writing today who does not rely, to a considerable extent, on his or her sympathetic Other—or others—to provide a balance point.

Now I was carrying "real" poems around in my head, struggling with them while still performing all the homely tasks of housekeeping. I think I was aided in this process by my early rote training. From grammar school on, I had been required in various classrooms to memorize poems, passages from John Greenleaf Whittier, Shakespeare, the Sermon on the Mount, Yeats, Housman. To this day, I require students to memorize eight to ten poems a semester for their inner library. A poem you are writing is easiest of all to remember. You can pull off the highway to make the revisions you have been chewing on. You can creep into the bathroom at 2 A.M. to scribble addenda.

By the end of the fifties there were a dozen serious literary magazines in my recipe box, again gleaned from the back pages of *The Writer* magazine. Some of these, miraculously, were beginning to take notice of me.

I wish I had kept a record of those early publications in the so-called "little" magazines. I remember one in particular, *The New Orleans Poetry Journal,* which has long since become extinct, and how hospitable the editor, Richard Ashman, was to neophytes. He wrote words of encouragement on the bottom of rejection slips, asked to see more work and again more. *Beloit Poetry Journal* was another cordial outlet. Then came *The Antioch Review* and *Contact* and *Audience* and *Accent.* I think *The Hudson Review* was my first big breakthrough into the world of the literary quarterlies.

I wish, too, that I had kept some sort of journal during the years of serious, warring, loving, almost violently productive workshops with Holmes and George Starbuck and Sexton and Samuel Albert. For by now we were meeting in one another's houses and continued to do so until John Holmes's death in 1962. We struck sparks off one another, spoke harshly, repented by way of letters mailed the morning after; encroached shamelessly on one another's apportioned time—here, Sexton was the prime offender; meddled and interfered, rewrote whole lines of one another's poems—here, Starbuck was clearly the front-runner; stayed on much too late out of pure sociability—this was Sam Albert's métier; took forever, striking matches and puffing on an overstuffed pipe as a considered dodge between statements—this was John Holmes. And we were noisy.

By then, with three children stuffed in a little Cape Cod house, my husband was in the throes of expanding upstairs, building a fourth bedroom out over the attached garage. Each time the children saw me setting out cups and glasses on a workshop evening, they would suspiciously ask, "Company? Who's coming?" On learning the truth, they groaned in unison. "The poets! Oh, no! Now we'll never get any sleep. Can we go sleep in the room over the garage?"

These are the humble confessions of a woman poet looking back over several decades. It seems to me that I spent the first half of my life trying to find the fulcrum between wife- and motherhood and the exigencies of my calling. Once I got over that early siege of poetic apocalyptic thoughts, I found myself drawing heavily on domestic experience. Many of my first poems came up out of dailiness to form what I have since come to call "tribal" poems—poems of family, of connectedness, of blood relation and bonding. For example, the following small poem, written in 1957 or 1958, and published in that first book, *Halfway*.

NIGHTMARE

This dwelt in me who does not know me now,
Where in her labyrinth I cannot follow
Advance to be recognized, displace her terror;
I hold my heartbeat on my lap and cannot comfort her.

Tonight she is condemned to cry out wolf
Or werewolf, and it echoes in the gulf
And no one comes to cradle cold Narcissus;
The first cell that divided separates us.

My book *Nurture* contains a section titled "More Tribal Poems"; now the tribe has increased to embrace a grandchild. But from first cell to last, we are all part of the continuum.

In the middle to late fifties, I had begun to write children's books on the side as an antidote to some of the books my own children seemed to prefer above all others. I particularly remember a treacly affair put out by the Junket Rennet Custard Company, and how I came to loathe being asked to read it aloud night after night to an addicted four-year-old.

Writing for children picked up on the versifying skills I had acquired writing for the slicks and newspaper columns. It was fun to work in rhyme, giving imagination a free rein to invent situations but controlling the material metrically. Since I undertook these original stories for internal circulation only, as it were, there was little ego involved. For the rennet-custard fancier I invented a character named Sebastian John Alexander Brown. To everyone's astonishment, Putnam bought the story and then invited me to write four more books, based on the seasons and written within the confines of a limited vocabulary. I chose to rhyme them as well, which I thought would enhance the challenge.

I came to Putnam's through the good offices of an agent named Diarmuid Russell, a distant friend of a distant friend of the parent of a college chum. He graciously agreed to look at the manuscript of a totally unknown would-be writer who had to learn how to pronounce his name. Diarmuid, son of the Irish poet A.E., was a famous New York literary figure. I was enormously in awe of him and he was enormously kind to me. He took me to lunch in Manhattan, downing four martinis to the one that made my head spin, typed all his own notes to me on a cranky manual machine with erratic margins, and represented me until his death although I never earned him the kind of return on his investment in me that his famous, mostly male, authors achieved.

The year before my first children's book was published, thanks to John Holmes and my musty master's degree, I was also launched in academe, teaching freshman composition, part time, to the phys ed majors and dental technicians at Tufts. We women in the department were not permitted to instruct the liberal arts candidates on the dubious grounds that we were part time (so were several of the male instructors) and, obviously, female. It didn't seem fair, but it certainly conformed to the order of the day, and we did not dispute it. We lobbied instead for a ladies' room, as it was called, in the English Department building, and this much was conceded us.

My teaching salary was $1,500 per annum. Each of the four children's books I wrote the following year earned me a $500 advance. I was an important wage earner.

All this was long ago—in another country, as we are fond of saying—but what I remember keenly from that period was the constant juggling act I had to perform in order to clear any space at all for my writing. I tried to establish a schedule in which I sat at my desk while the kids were at school, and this was not hard to do, provided I put the telephone in a drawer with a pillow over it. We did not then have phone jacks one could disconnect at will. Sometimes, if I was pressed, I tried to work while the children were at home. I cajoled, I threatened, I ordered them into separate rooms. On one such occasion, I saw an envelope being pushed under my door. Intrigued, I opened it. There, written in a thinly disguised foreign hand, was the following: "Dear Mrs. Kumin, I think your stories are awful and your poems are worse. I hope they never sell. Signed, A Well-Wisher."

Margaret Walker, in an essay in the first volume of *The Writer on Her Work,* speaks for all of us, white and black, acclaimed and struggling, when she says, "What are the critical decisions I must make as a woman, as a writer? They are questions of compromise, and of guilt."

I like to think that a little guilt makes the world go round, and that the ability to compromise deserves high marks, for it is a learned skill. The life inside my poems was worth whatever it took to get there: guilt and compromise, tenacity, an inner secrecy that hid behind the facade of suburban housewife, Girl Scout leader, swimming instructor, chauffeur, and straw boss.

"You drive like a man," men said admiringly back in the fifties if you threaded your way through rush-hour traffic, took shortcuts and chances, got them to the airport on time. "You write like a man," they said, paying you the highest compliment in their lexicon if your poem was androgynous and intellectual, that is, eschewed domestic life.

Two events—the coming of the women's movement and the establishment of what was then called the Radcliffe Institute for Independent Study—saved me from lifelong imitation of male models. In 1961, the first year of the Institute, I received a grant and an office in the little frame building on Mt. Auburn Street. The grant was not munificent, but it covered babysitters. The office was symbolic (I seldom used it); it said, You Have Earned This.

The rest is history. I cannot believe, looking back, how old I have grown, how long ago was the acute phase of the struggle to be taken seriously as a writer, first by myself, and then by the world of editors. The gender gap is still there but no longer yawns as an all but unleapable chasm. Women poets need no longer hide behind first initials. Editors of national magazines no longer reply that they loved your poem, but they published a woman last month and thus you are *de trop*. And while a number of major male poets continue to stammer when asked what women poets they read with interest, before coming up with the name of the long dead and safely buried *Emily,* I am delighted by the comments of Anthony Hecht, Stanley

Kunitz, and William Stafford, for example, on the works of Alicia
Ostriker, Linda Pastan, Carolyn Kizer, and others.

I love what I read by women. They are in the process of telling
"the world's best-kept secret:/Merely the private lives of one-half of
humanity," as Kizer puts it. I turn to Oates, Oles, Ostriker, Lever-
tov, Rich, Stone, Swenson; to Adams, Hoffman, Godwin, Morrison,
Silko, Tyler, Atwood, Drabble, Munro, Walker; to Lessing and
Gordimer and easily three dozen more. I am drawn to them by way
of affirmation, confirmation, a sharing of insights, a drawing out of
disagreements and discrepancies. It is all part of my right-to-know.

Caring, as I said once in a poem, is seamless. "We must love one
another or die," Auden declared, in a poem he later renounced but
could not expunge. Ideally, caring is genderless, along with equal
pay and equal opportunity. In the real world, however, we are still
the primary care-givers; this is the world we live in and must write
about.

TRAVELLING WRITER

JAN
MORRIS

In my heart I resist the title of this book, or rather its implication: namely that it matters whether a writer is male or female. I believe the fount of art to be beyond gender, just as I believe the human soul itself to be housed in a particular physique merely for practical purposes of reproduction—slotted along the continuum that is, in my view, the true measure of sex. The so-called war between the sexes seems to me a trumped-up conflict, presently to be resolved: and I suspect that the very distinction between masculine and femi-nine will one day be of purely functional significance.

But having lived my own life partly as a man, partly as a woman, I recognize of course how powerfully, in our own time, the circum-stance of gender affects one's work as a writer: and I admit that at the core of everything I have done myself, somewhere between the lines of all my books, lies the fact of my own particular and peculiar status in the present state of sex.

. . .

Take for a start the workaday, humdrum aspects of the writer's life. I am a travelling writer—not a travel writer, a category I reject, but a writer who travels. That I write about place is almost incidental to my vocation. I am really an essayist, often of an all too protracted kind, but it so happens that the Second World War, by making me a traveller whether I wanted it or not, provided me with a particular range of subject matter—the matter of place, which I have manipulated ever since in works of memoir, description, history, and fiction. If chance had given me a more domestic role in life, I have no doubt that the basic material of my essays would have been altogether different, and I might have launched myself from the start into miniatures or abstractions.

Be that as it may, destiny made me a travelling writer, with all the addictions that such a calling implies: restless addictions, footloose addictions, a taste for the solitary, and an appetite for things colorful, quirky, and exciting. After the British Army and Oxford University I spent a decade as a foreign correspondent, and this soon instilled in me, as it instills in most practitioners of the trade, a cynical disregard for fame, power, and consequence: but it also disqualified me once and for all for the routines and preoccupations of life at home.

So I wander always, torn between the places I love the best of all, my own corner of Wales, and the kaleidoscopic variety of everywhere else: between the people I love the best, my family, and the inexhaustible allure of new faces, languages, styles, and manners of thought. It is a *wrenched* kind of life, a perpetual dichotomy, a periodical trauma, but I am certainly not complaining: if this is neurosis, you can keep your normalcy.

It is however a demanding existence, stressful and just occasionally dangerous, and at literary festivals especially I am often asked if it has become easier for me, or more difficult, since I made my shift along the gauge of sex. In some ways, I have to reply, more difficult, because physically it is obviously riskier, even now, for a woman to travel alone in the world with the intention of writing about it. One is more vulnerable than a man, more conspicuous too, and technically this has sometimes been a handicap to me. Aspects of life that I was once free to explore are now more generally denied me, and I have occasionally regretted it, when the dim lights and loud music of a dubious tavern beckon, or I am disbarred from entering some fascinatingly old-school club.

But not often. I have hated nightlife always, and seldom in fact pine for leather-backed chairs and gentlemanly tradition. Besides, I set against these lesser disadvantages the assets of travelling as a woman. The chief and most obvious of these is the fact that among the human species, as among most of the animals, the female is not generally perceived as threatening. Novelists and New Yorkers may scoff, but in general it is true, and the solitary woman traveller raises far fewer suspicions, finds far fewer doors closed against her, than does a wandering man.

More positively, too, the woman travelling writer can know that more than half of humanity is likely to be actually on her side— cheering her on! When Kipling wrote about "sisters under the skin," he was in his allusive way enunciating a great truth: that on the whole—and God knows, with exceptions—women are kinder to women than men are to men. You must take my word for this, as one who has experienced both relationships, and you must believe me too that for a writer especially this grand freemasonry around the world infinitely outweighs a woman's vulnerability as a traveller.

Twenty years ago I would have said that on the other hand the woman was hampered by male inability to take her seriously. I used to feel it myself, when I first began to travel as a woman, and found my opinions disregarded and my questions patronizingly set aside. No longer. It is the great triumph of the feminist movement that the intellectual equality of women is now all but universally recognized (if not invariably, especially when it comes to equal pay or opportunity, admitted . . .).

Anyway all this is ancillary to the writer's craft and purpose, which is above all self-generating and internal. I don't believe a sensibility depends upon gender, and I think I write in the way I write not because I am male, female, both, or neither, but simply because I am myself: *"le style est l'homme même,"* said de Buffon long ago, but he meant *l'homme,* I do not doubt, in shorthand for humanity.

Sensibility however is a different thing from experience, and the experience of our gender, while it may not affect our style, certainly affects our responses. In my own case the anomalies of my sex have powerfully affected, without doubt, the way I have looked at the world, besides the way I have lived in it. I expect in some respects they have distorted or weakened my reactions, but I prefer to look upon the bright side, and contemplate their benefits instead.

I think they made me, from the start, one of life's outsiders. This would be a weakness for writers of other kinds, but it has been good for me. The essence of my work, whether it deals with the past or the present, whether it is fact or fiction, is detachment—not alienation or estrangement, merely standing separate. Actually detachment of a kind is endemic to the tradition of English writing to which I feel myself, though actually Anglo-Welsh, to belong: the classic detachment of the English abroad, amounting very nearly to aloofness and exemplified in the work of such masters of my own genre as Emily Eden or Alexander Kinglake. American writers about place have more generally felt the urge to get within the skin of the people they are observing: English writers have preferred to watch from a safe distance, through a screen of irony.

More fundamentally, and conversely, I like to think my peculiar sexuality has widened my empathies. If I feel separate from everyone, I feel close to everyone too. Starting with men and women, many of whose varied emotions I have actually shared, I have been able, as I grow older, to extend my range of fellow-feeling: to animals, for instance, to nations, even to inanimate objects. I believe in the absolute equality before God of all living things, slug to dolphin. I do not recognize the crime of treason, having long ago reached the conclusion that nationality, like loyalty, should be purely a matter of choice. I do not feel in the least foolish in apologizing to a table, if I trip over its leg, or jollying along a recalcitrant automobile with encouraging words.

There is a smugness to these attitudes, I know, and a sentimentality too: but then the faults of a writer, as well as the virtues, contribute for better or for worse to the nature of her art.

And on the whole, smug, sentimental, or just a little crazy, I feel myself to be a kind of portent. I believe the conjunction of my self and my work to be a sign of reconciliation—a minuscule sign, Heaven knows, and one apparent perhaps only to myself, but still to my mind a promise of things to come. Long ago the philosopher Teilhard de Chardin conceived the idea of "infurling," an infinitely slow, almost imperceptible coming together of the world and its beings. I see in myself and my work one all but imperceptible confirmation of his vision: and I believe that in a couple of centuries, when people read this book, they will wonder at the primitive nature of our own times, when art could still be collated with gender at all.

HEARING VOICES

LINDA
HOGAN

When Barbara McClintock was awarded a Nobel Prize for her work on gene transposition in corn plants, the most striking thing about her was that she made her discoveries by listening to what the corn spoke to her, by respecting the life of the corn and "letting it come."

McClintock says she learned "the stories" of the plants. She "heard" them. She watched the daily green journeys of growth from earth toward sky and sun. She knew her plants in the way a healer or mystic would have known them, from the inside, the inner voices of corn and woman speaking to one another.

As an Indian woman, I come from a long history of people who have listened to the language of this continent, people who have known that corn grows with the songs and prayers of the people, that it has a story to tell, that the world is alive. Both in oral traditions and in mythology—the true language of inner life— account after account tells of the stones giving guidance, the trees singing, the corn telling of inner earth, the dragonfly offering up a tongue. This is true in the European traditions as well: Psyche received direction from the reeds and the ants, Orpheus knew the languages of earth, animals, and birds.

This intuitive and common language is what I seek for my writing, work in touch with the mystery and force of life, work that speaks a few of the many voices around us, and it is important to me that McClintock listened to the voices of corn. It is important to the continuance of life that she told the truth of her method and that it reminded us all of where our strength, our knowing, and our sustenance come from.

It is also poetry, this science, and I note how often scientific theories lead to the world of poetry and vision, theories telling us how atoms that were stars have been transformed into our living, breathing bodies. And in these theories, or maybe they should be called stories, we begin to understand how we are each many people, including the stars we once were, and how we are in essence the earth and the universe, how what we do travels clear around the earth and returns. In a single moment of our living, there is our ancestral and personal history, our future, even our deaths planted in us and already growing toward their fulfillment. The corn plants are there, and like all the rest we are forever merging our borders with theirs in the world collective.

Our very lives might depend on this listening. In the Chernobyl nuclear accident, the wind told the story that was being suppressed by the people. It gave away the truth. It carried the story of danger to other countries. It was a poet, a prophet, a scientist.

Sometimes, like the wind, poetry has its own laws speaking for the life of the planet. It is a language that wants to bring back together what the other words have torn apart. It is the language of life speaking through us about the sacredness of life.

This life speaking life is what I find so compelling about the work of poets such as Ernesto Cardenal, who is also a priest and was the Nicaraguan Minister of Culture. He writes: "The armadilloes are very happy with this government. . . . Not only humans desired liberation/the whole ecology wanted it." Cardenal has also written "The Parrots," a poem about caged birds who were being sent to the United States as pets for the wealthy, how the cages were opened, the parrots allowed back into the mountains and jungles, freed like the people, "and sent back to the land we were pulled from."

How we have been pulled from the land! And how poetry has worked hard to set us free, uncage us, keep us from split tongues that mimic the voices of our captors. It returns us to our land. Poetry is a string of words that parades without a permit. It is a lockbox of words to put an ear to as we try to crack the safe of language, listening for the right combination, the treasure inside. It is life resonating. It is sometimes called Prayer, Soothsaying, Complaint, Invocation, Proclamation, Testimony, Witness. Writing is and does all these things. And like that parade, it is illegitimately insistent on going its own way, on being part of the miracle of life, telling the story about what happened when we were cosmic dust, what it means to be stars listening to our human atoms.

But don't misunderstand me. I am not just a dreamer. I am also the practical type. A friend's father, watching the United States stage another revolution in another Third World country, said, "Why doesn't the government just feed people and then let the political chips fall where they may?" He was right. It was easy, obvious, even financially more reasonable to do that, to let democracy be chosen because it feeds hunger. I want my writing to be that simple, that clear and direct. Likewise, I feel it is not enough for me just to write, but I need to live it, to be informed by it. I have found over the years that my work has more courage than I do. It has more wisdom. It teaches me, leads me places I never knew I was heading. And it is about a new way of living, of being in the world.

I was on a panel recently where the question was raised whether we thought literature could save lives. The audience, book people, smiled expectantly with the thought. I wanted to say, Yes, it saves lives. But I couldn't speak those words. It saves spirits maybe, hearts.

It changes minds, but for me writing is an incredible privilege. When I sit down at the desk, there are other women who are hungry, homeless. I don't want to forget that, that the world of matter is still there to be reckoned with. This writing is a form of freedom most other people do not have. So, when I write, I feel a responsibility, a commitment to other humans and to the animal and plant communities as well.

Still, writing has changed me. And there is the powerful need we all have to tell a story, each of us with a piece of the whole pattern to complete. As Alice Walker says, We are all telling part of the same story, and as Sharon Olds has said, Every writer is a cell on the body politic of America.

Another Nobel Prize laureate is Betty William, a Northern Ireland co-winner of the 1977 Peace Prize. I heard her speak about how, after witnessing the death of children, she stepped outside in the middle of the night and began knocking on doors and yelling, behaviors that would have earned her a diagnosis of hysteria in our own medical circles. She knocked on doors that might have opened with weapons pointing in her face, and she cried out, "What kind of people have we become that we would allow children to be killed on our streets?" Within four hours the city was awake, and there were sixteen thousand names on petitions for peace. Now, that woman's work is a lesson to those of us who deal with language, and to those of us who are dealt into silence. She used language to begin the process of peace. This is the living, breathing power of the word. It is poetry. So are the names of those who signed the petitions. Maybe it is this kind of language that saves lives.

Writing begins for me with survival, with life and with freeing life, saving life, speaking life. It is work that speaks what can't be easily said. It originates from a compelling desire to live and be alive. For me, it is sometimes the need to speak for other forms of life, to take the side of human life, even our sometimes frivolous living, and our grief-filled living, our joyous living, our violent living, busy living, our peaceful living. It is about possibility. It is based in the world of matter. I am interested in how something small turns into an image that is large and strong with resonance, where the ordinary becomes beautiful. I believe the divine, the magic, is here in the weeds at our feet, unacknowledged. What a world this is. Where else could water rise up to the sky, turn into snow crystals, magnificently brought together, fall from the sky all around us, pile up billions deep, and catch the small sparks of sunlight as they return again to water?

These acts of magic happen all the time; in Chaco Canyon, my sister has seen a kiva, a ceremonial room in the earth, that is in the center of the canyon. This place has been uninhabited for what seems like forever. It has been without water. In fact, there are theories that the ancient people disappeared when they journeyed after water. In the center of it a corn plant was growing. It was all alone and it had been there since the ancient ones, the old ones who came before us all, those people who wove dog hair into belts, who witnessed the painting of flute players on the seeping canyon walls, who knew the stories of corn. And there was one corn plant growing out of the holy place. It planted itself yearly. With no water, no person to care for it, no overturning of the soil, this corn plant rises up to tell its story, and that's what this poetry is.

A QUESTION MARK
ENGRAVED ON MY EYELIDS

ELENA
PONIATOWSKA

I write in order to belong. My family on my mother's side (my great-grandmother, grandmother, and mother) were always traveling. They had lost their land during the Mexican Revolution, but they still had enough money to live in Biarritz, then in Paris, and later in "Fairlight," England. (I would much rather have called it "Wuthering Heights" but "Fairlight" it was, sweet and *comme il faut*.) They would travel from Karlsbad to Lausanne, from Marienbad to Vichy, to "take the waters." They would get off at a station, stay for a week, then get back on the train. They would see the switchman grow smaller and smaller, his lantern turn into a firefly. My grandmother's house was filled with portraits of Goethe and Wagner, and with books in German; she loved Germany. Mamy-Grand, who was a very young widow, was called "the Madonna of Sleeping Cars," because she took so many, so very many trains. She always dressed in black, her white milky throat and décolletage illuminating the blackness of her veils and *crêpes de Chine*. Later, in Mexico, I would pause on Venustiano Carranza Street, before the window of a shop that sold outfits for a woman's ideal state: widow-hood. I never tried on a wedding gown, but I did try on widow's clothes. Widows used to go around the way the poet Jaime Sabines would like them to: "There is one way, my love, that you could make me completely happy: die." Now widows are not even merry.

The traveling companions of Elena Iturbe de Amor were three little girls in ruffles, petticoats, ribbons, and hats, their little faces lost amidst billows of embroidered cloth: Biche, Lydia, and Paula—my mother. The nanny who stands behind them in the photographs was also covered in starch and crepes. Mamy-Grand would carry her samovar with her (because my great-grandmother, Elena Idaroff, was Russian), as well as her silk sheets to put on the hotel beds. It's not that we were gypsies, although we do have some of that in our blood, it's just that we seemed not to belong. Biche still wears strings of pearls dangling about her stomach and her chains remind me of railroad tracks.

From sweet France, the land of the handkerchief-size gardens (*lieu commun*) and of tender vegetables that fit in the palm of your hand (peas are also pearls), I arrived in an enormous plain surrounded by mountains and live volcanoes, traversed by buzzards that would circle around and then suddenly swoop down to feed off the carcass of some skinny little donkey. A land of corn, hard, yellow corn, like large teeth, that women grind on a stone into tortillas. Not just the *metate* and *molcajete*—the grinding stone and mortar—but many things in Mexico were stonelike: the expressions on people's faces and the windowless houses that looked like small pyramids all curved into themselves. As a young girl, it seemed my eyes would burst trying to reach as far as the horizon. The stern, dark-green magueys would come marching toward us, goose-stepping like Ger-man soldiers. It was a fearful and splendid country; from up high one could see a little train crossing the valley with its colored-pencil smoke, a lone toy amidst the vastness of the landscape. I knew that I wanted to be part of it, to step into the painting, stand on the mountaintop, be the girl on the edge of the precipice and have a twentieth-century José María Velasco paint me there.

One way of belonging was to listen, to see faces, to take them into oneself, to observe laps, hands. I liked to spend time in the warm kitchen, fragrant with spices; the toasted chiles would make us cough; the boiling milk was always on the verge of spilling over. I would follow Felicitas to the rooftop (rooftops are the realm of servants), where she would wash her long, long black hair with "chichicastle," a small, green, foaming herb. For years I would go with her to the market. I would sit on park benches to wait for her while she kissed her boyfriend. They were such long kisses! I was enormously curious about the servants' lives, and about the villages they left behind to come to Mexico City. One of them, Epifania, had epileptic seizures that terrified me, especially because she didn't want anyone to know about them. Later, when I read Dostoyevski, I was in familiar territory, so I loved him all the more.

I absorbed Mexico through the maids. A system still persists in Latin America which consists of privileged people having at their beck and call the poorest of the poor. In some space within their bodies, perhaps in their unbraided hair, maids are extraordinarily free because they expect nothing; they leave the minute they want to. And alongside their everyday life of garlic and onions, they have a mysterious and magical life, which grows in an inaccessible, arrogant terrain that can be as haughty as the realm of their masters.

In my country today, one doesn't have to be very wealthy in order to have the services of someone who doubles as washing machine, dryer, garbage disposal, salad mixer, vacuum cleaner, and bed-maker, who responds with a human voice, and who even says thank you when she gets her meager salary. When I was a child, the servants' lives and miracles fascinated me, because they didn't keep the distances that European maîtres d'hôtel and chefs do. On the contrary, I discovered Mexico through them, and not even Bernal Díaz del Castillo had better guides. Surrounded by Malinches (Ma-

lintzín, the Indian woman who gave herself to the conqueror Her-
nán Cortés, thus betraying her race), I was able to enter an unknown
world, that of poverty and its palliatives: teas and potions that could
ward off even the pain of the soul; herbs for stale air; eucalyptus to
clear the lungs; the bitter *tolache,* a tea which they say drove the
empress Charlotte mad, when she tried in vain to have Maximilian's
death sentence commuted. The same Maximilian that my mother
loves, because not only did he say "Soldiers, aim at my heart," but he
also saw the deep blue sky of Querétaro, found it beautiful, and said
that it was a good thing to die on such a day.

Without realizing it the maids provided me with a version of
Benito Juárez; they were all like Benito Juárez. Like him they vin-
dicated themselves: "Dirty foreigners." Like him they defended
Mexico, as stubborn as mules. Like him they had no roof of their
own and had eaten only poor people's food, and for me, a girl raised
on French mashed potatoes, discovering them meant entering into
"the other." I have always wanted to lose myself in others, to belong
to other people, to be the same as them. It is always the others who
are right, who hold the key to the enigma. Since then, my capacity
for entering the lives of other people has been unlimited, to the point
that I could no longer hold myself back, define my limits, much less
define myself. To this day, if I ask so many questions, it is because I
don't have a single answer. I believe I will die like this, still searching, with a question mark engraved on my eyelids.

Perhaps this sense of not belonging made me a writer. As for the
questions, I have interviewed more than a thousand people, from
Henry Moore to Luis Buñuel, from Barry Goldwater to André
Malraux, from Gabriel García Márquez to William Golding. *What,
when, how, where:* the answers are always surprising, because in Latin
America reality surpasses fiction. Journalism traps one. It fills one's
head; an internal trepidation makes one sweat ink. Cyril Connolly
was right when he said that art needs clean hands.

To write in Latin America has a different meaning than it has in the United States or in Europe. I suppose the same happens in Africa. Latin America invades, possesses, interferes, gets into the smallest crack. Latin America is always out there, behind the window, watching, spying, ready to jump. The street enters through the door, people find their way in, look at you while you are sleeping, eating, or making love. The path is public. In great American cities, everyone has something to do, people go somewhere, walk quickly, never turn their heads to look at their neighbor. In Latin America, in Mexico, no one has anywhere to go. Thousands and thousands of people with nothing for themselves. Nothing. Not a single opportunity. Their empty hands hang near their bodies, in front of their mouths, or on top of their knees, their waiting hands without any use. All this human energy is there, wasted. They look, they wait, they look, they doze, they wait again. Nobody loves them, nobody misses them, they are not needed anywhere. They are nobody. They do not exist. So much to do in the world, and there is no place for them, so much lost energy. There is no one to tell them, let's get up, let's get going, let's save, let's build. Outside my window, the multitude is always present, ready to burst in. Life is very resistant. People—the same cannon fodder that nourishes great universal misfortunes, "the wretched of the earth," as Frantz Fanon called them. Suddenly, during an earthquake, one of them saves a life. We have no idea who he is, what his name is, no way to thank him, he doesn't expect to be thanked, we will never see him again, he saved our lives, or murdered us—maybe it doesn't matter, maybe it's the same—he is there, latent, frightfully present.

In the United States, I suppose that people are in the back of a writer's head, in the back of their minds. In Europe also, they sit there waiting to be picked up as characters in a story, in a novel. In Mexico, people are settled in the front of our minds; they never go away, they are always waiting, expecting. Isn't it then an absurdity to write? María Luisa Erreguerena, a young Mexican writer who wrote a delightful and witty story, "The Day God Got in Bed with

Me," doesn't write anymore. She became a doctor.

For instance: there was a football game in Mexico City. People tried to get in, they were crushed to death in the tunnels. A father came out, the corpse of his son in his arms. Before, between El Salvador and Honduras, there was a football war. Because of a game, the army of El Salvador invaded Honduras, the air force bombed four cities, and, in retaliation, Honduras tried to penetrate El Salvador; thousands of men were killed.

The people of Honduras and El Salvador are completely alike, same height, same complexion, same poverty, same color; all of them are accustomed to misfortune. During the student movement in 1968 (the same as in Berkeley, Paris, Nancy, Tokyo, Prague) more than four hundred Mexicans were killed. In Latin America, stadiums are built for games, but they are also used as concentration camps, as jails, for public trials, and, in 1985, after a devastating earthquake, they were transformed into morgues where people could go and claim the bodies of their dead relatives. This isn't to say that we Mexicans have the monopoly on all the sufferings in the world and that I think of myself as the universal widow of all afflictions, faithful to my youth's vocation. But it is true that it is different to be a writer in Latin America and in Africa than in other countries.

It is difficult to follow up a multitude but in my huge country no one waits to become part of a novel. People jump like rabbits into vowels and consonants and they stick their ears out. And their teeth. The first time I saw Jesusa, I knew she was going to eat up all my words. In 1963, I had what I believe was the fundamental meeting of my life, with Jesusa Palancares,* the protagonist of my book *Hasta no verte Jesús mío*. She was less than five feet tall and the years had made her smaller, rounded her shoulders. She had lost her beautiful hair, for which she once had been called "Reina Xochitl" (Queen Flower) by the soldiers of the Revolution. There were brown stains

*Not her real name.

on her hands; she said they were due to her liver, but I rather thought they were from the passing of time. With time, men and women are gradually covered by mountain ranges and depressions, hills and deserts. Jesusa increasingly resembled the earth; she was a mound that walks, a clay pitcher dried in the sun. When I met her she was fierce. "You say you want to talk with me? With me? Look, I work and if I don't work I don't eat. I haven't got time to chat, least of all with strangers."

It was true. She didn't need anyone, she was enough for herself, she completed herself, alone, she was her other half. One of her main topics was always "the rent" and she moved out many times. On each occasion she ended up farther away because the city tosses out its poor, getting rid of them, pushing them out, throwing them away as far as possible. Her last home had no drainage, no water, no light.

I think about her with reverence. I love her. I talk to her inside my heart. Inside my head. My breasts love her; because of her I also love being a woman, I who, at age fifteen, wanted to be a man. Jesusa gave me a hard time at first. I won her over little by little. She began to tell me the story of her nomadic life in the Revolution. She was part of a multitude. I asked her seventy-seven thousand questions. She answered patiently, then she became irritated. She just couldn't understand how someone with schooling could be so ignorant, so slow to catch on. She was right. She didn't like the final version of the novel; she asked me not to bother her with that fucking thing again and, above all, not to put her name in it. Jesusa led the way. Neither of us insisted, neither of us forced the other to say anything. We never referred directly to the act of love. I asked for no explanations. She knew humanity well and had no faith in me:

"The interest is yours, not mine. You'll come to see me as long as you are able to get something out of me. When you don't need me anymore I'll never see the likes of you again." One night she repeated: "Some day you will come and you won't find me; you'll find only the wind. This day will come and there will be no one to give you any information, and you will think that everything has been a lie. It's true, it's a lie that we are here, the stories they tell on the radio are lies, the neighbors tell lies, and it's a lie that you are going to miss me. If I am of no use anymore, what the hell are you going to miss? And in the factory also. Who will miss me if I'm not even going to say goodbye?"

Jesusa greatly influenced my life, because she has never asked anything of anyone. She has never been a subordinate although her life was so hard. As she demanded a great deal of herself, she taught me to follow her down the road. We are here in order to serve. We are sent here to earth by God, and if we are bad, we will return time and time again in different forms to atone for our guilt. Jesusa used to say that she must have been a very bad, drunken man who had abused women in an earlier life, in order to suffer as much as she did in her last reincarnation.

I would like to return to earth because I love life. I would like to gaze, even from afar, on the grandchildren of my grandchildren and on everyone's grandchildren, to see the trees, especially the "pirules" (American pepper trees) and the "sabinos" (Mexican cypresses), the city square of the Zócalo "where the greatest storm fits," the sea on the coast of Oaxaca, the turtles that Francisco Toledo paints, his grasshoppers, the rabbit that laughs, and the fox that pokes fun at us all. I would like to go back holding Jesusa's hand, both of us young and strong, able to walk the whole road. I would like to see her smoking a "Farito" slowly, very slowly, holding it between her thumb and her index finger; I would like to offer her an aged tequila, a glass of water left out in the night air, a green lemon.

I feel that I didn't do her justice with *Hasta no verte Jesús mío;* I obeyed her, faithful to the point of exacerbation, hanging on each of her gestures like a person in love. The images that I have of her are painful, they wound me. Because of her I underwent a process of self-examination. I had the feeling that I was stealing her words and that, in exchange for the treasure that she was unknowingly placing in my hands, I would not even be able to offer a portrait of her essence. No one on earth has given me what Jesusa offered me. No one of my social class has ever said to me what I have heard from Jesusa, no one with her features, no one with her wisdom—the wisdom of corn and wind. While she picks up sticks and paper and old rags and bricks to build her house, we debate on the psychiatrist's couch. To be a troop follower, a *soldadera,* is to walk with the soldiers, to prepare food, to participate in the campaign. Jesusa, for example, gallops next to her husband, Pedro Aguilar, and while he shoots, she loads his Mauser. When he dies, she is the one who shoots. She gives us fulminating images, unforgettable ones of what it means to fight. In Mexico, life isn't worth anything and when he falls off his horse, she doesn't notice it at first, so brutally simple is death. "I was still handing him his Mauser and since he didn't take it, I looked over but Pedro was not on his horse anymore."

In Mexico, we are accustomed to calling poor Mexicans "Indians." Indians, the Mazahuas, the Nahuas, the Mayas, the Otomíes who sell chewing gum in the streets; Indians for being indigenous and carrying out the humblest tasks. In this sense Jesusa is Indian: she comes from Oaxaca, she's dark skinned, and for years she worked as a maid; her parents were peasants and the land holds no secrets for her, although she never went back to her province. In contrast to Mexican women peasants she does not remain silent; she speaks out. In contrast with other Mexican women peasants, she had no children of her own, but she picked up stray children and dogs in the streets, fed them and taught them how to work, hit them to teach them "education" like she had been taught. And loved them.

Jesusa led me to social problems and to my writing books like *Massacre in Mexico,* about the student movement in 1968; *Strong Is the Silence,* the story of land seizures in the states of Morelos and Guerrero, and peasant struggles for land, political prisoners and hunger strikes; *Nothing, No One,* against the Mexican government, its incompetence and its corruption, and for the people's courage during the earthquake in 1985; and *It All Began on Sunday,* with drawings by Alberto Beltrán, a book on the holidays of the poor, their Sundays sitting in the streets watching the cars go by and, if they are lucky enough, riding on merry-go-rounds. Carefully I asked them questions, visited them in their crowded neighborhoods, watched their kites cross the sky in February, treated them like kites, because that's how testimonial literature is. It fills one with anxiety, with insecurity. One handles very fragile material, people's hearts; their names, which are their honor; their work; and their time. And one tries to turn it into memorable material. I never imagined that Jesusa would become a well-known literary character, nor did I foresee that *La noche de Tlatelolco* (*Massacre in Mexico*) would be read by the young. Books take on a life of their own and they find their own destiny. That is the sorcery of literature.

I have always walked. I think as I stroll along: How much of me there is in these faces that don't know me and that I don't know, how much of me in the subway, in the steps that pile up, one on top of the other, until they finally come out into the great, white spout of light, how much of me in the last, weary steps coming out, how much of me in the rain that forms puddles on the pavement, how much of me in the smell of wet wool, how much of me in the rusted steel sheets, how much of me in the Colonia del Valle-coyoacán buses that rush along until they crash and form part of the cosmos, in the graffiti on the walls, in the pavement, in the earth trod on a thousand times. How much of me in those worn-out benches, their paint flaking, how much in the hardware stores, in the little corner stores, how much in all those testosterone shots on those dusty pharmacy shelves, in those syringes that used to be boiled and that spread hepatitis, how much of me in the signs that used to hang all along San Juan de Letrán: "All types of venereal diseases treated," how much in the newspaper stands, in the Fountain of the Little Frogs, in the shoe-shine boxes, in the rickety trees—just like little sticks climbing up to the sky—in the man who sold electric shocks, in the old people's wrinkles, in the young people's legs.

The women in my family share a peculiarity, the absence that others call distraction. We are never really there. In her middle age, a doctor friend used to give Biche such tedious explanations that she claimed, "I don't listen to him. I think about something else." My mother has always thought about something else. For her, coming back to reality must be like stepping into a coffee grinder. I believe that my mother could only accept her suffering over her one son's death through her capacity for evasion and, especially, through her faith. My brother is better off in Heaven; who knows how things would have turned out for Jan if he had continued on earth. Wrapped in scarves, ethereal, with her long neck and her elusive gaze, my mother, the most beautiful of all women, is the one who most inspires my love, because I have never been able to reach her. Now, when she wants to give herself to me, I return her to her niche. No, no, don't do it. The curtain is lifted by the wind and I cover my eyes.

I have always responded to challenges, followed apocalyptical personalities, apostles, Rasputins, Joans of Arc who hear voices that come from Heaven, illuminated guides of humanity, holders of truth, priests. During my childhood I was marked by competition amid the worn desks, the purple ink of the government school in the south of France. I dutifully accepted the repressive atmosphere, even though inside myself I sensed something subversive that I would have to let out: a joy at daybreak, as if a sun were going to burst from my mouth. But when? How? One of the reasons why I married my husband was because he was an astronomer. He would explain to me what it all meant, he would tell me why we are here and where we are going, our reason for being. We would become, our three children and myself, part of his universe. We would belong. Once again, the problem of belonging.

I live to the rhythm of my country and I cannot remain on the sidelines. I want to be here. I want to be part of it. I want to be a witness. I want to walk arm in arm with it. I want to hear it more and more, to cradle it, to carry it like a medal on my chest. Activism is a constant element in my life, even though afterwards I anguish over not having written "my own things." Testimonial literature provides evidence of events that people would like to hide, denounces and therefore is political and part of a country in which everything remains to be done and documented.

Some Latin American writers inscribe our literature within a collective project. In this respect Carlos Monsiváis and I are just two more Mexicans out of the 84 million that now exist, and a smidgen of the 103 million that there will be by the year 2000. Our reality is therefore infinitesimal. It is barely a dot, the head of a pin within the sea of heads that covers our territory, like in that photograph of men in hats that Tina Modotti took during the 1920s, a sea of hats, a sea of heads, each head a world. Mexico between each person's ears. Mexico is a country of young people. Since 1980, one and a half million young people have entered the labor market, and our country has not created the twenty million jobs that are needed for the other unemployed and underemployed Mexicans. Even today, we know that there are fifteen million hungry people.

In spite of these voices, every morning in Mexico I get up to life without knowing what it is. Also to literature. Nor can I decipher the enigma of my country, nor that of my children, let alone everyone else's children. I have always had questions, and to this day, I don't have a single answer. I simply don't have any. I look for them in other people. In their words, in their acts, in the expressions on their faces. Sometimes at a party, some eyes will encounter mine, just a blink. I really loved the sidelong gaze, green and yellow like a parrot, that my father used to turn on me. My father was my son, just as today my son Mane is my father. Of Polish origin, he used to cry. Poles cry. Mexicans almost never cry. Machos never do. He loved my mother like the first Poniatowski loved Catherine the Great, who made him King of Poland in order to get rid of him. He wrote her passionate letters. "I don't want to be king, I want to be in your bed." Perhaps he wasn't a very good lover, but he was a gentle king. My father never knew how to ask anything of anyone. In Mexico his heroism was his secret. He never formed part of any chorus. One had to grasp him intuitively. It was on the piano that he expressed himself best, but at age seventy he stopped believing even in musical notes. When he died I knew that he was inside me, that I would become him, as all my dead are in me.

What will Felipe and Paula do? What will they be? What can one do with this bundle of uncertainties that knocks around inside one's head?

I have always been drawn to characters like Jesusa Palancares. María Sabina, the one who performed the ceremony of the sacred mushrooms (LSD in Oaxaca), Juan Perez Jolote (the Chamula peasant from Chiapas), Demetrio Vallejo (the railroad leader), all popular heroes, even if they are not recognized. I admire them because of their wisdom and the way they impart it, with great patience, great prudence, with respect for the ignorance of the person who asks the questions. That the poorest Mexicans don't deserve their ruling class is a truth that leaps out at once.

For Stephen Spender, the Spanish Civil War in 1936 was a war of classes, on an international scale; the capitalistic class, backed by international imperialism, against the democratic will of 80 percent of the Spanish people. In 1990, the reality of Latin America is not very different from Spender's Spain. In Latin America, wars are class wars, on one side the oligarchy linked to the military class and the great capital and, on the other, the poor people, the ones who have nothing to lose. Fear of communism in 1936 is still flagrant in 1990. And more absurd, more mediocre.

Writers in Latin America live in a reality that is extraordinarily demanding. Surprisingly, our answer to these demands protects and develops our individuality. I feel I am not alone in trying to give their voice to those who don't have it.

In 1979, for instance, Marta Traba published *Homerica latina*. Marta Traba was a very sophisticated and well-known art critic, a sort of "enfant terrible" at the Museum of Modern Art in Colombia. She was brilliant, original, and feared. She died in a plane crash in Aeropuerto Barajas in 1980. To me, *Homerica latina* was a surprise, and a still greater surprise was *Conversación al sur* (*Mothers and Shadows*), about the political situation and the mothers of the Plaza de Mayo in Argentina. Marta Traba had suddenly changed. Multitudes took over. Multitudes invaded her. No art museum could close the doors. *Homerica latina* is a novel in which the characters are the losers of our continent, those who pick up the garbage and live from it, the inhabitants of the slums, the masses who trample on each other to see the pope, those who travel on the crowded buses, those who cover their heads with straw hats, those who—like Jesusa—have nothing to lose except their lives. They take their dead children to be blessed and photographed so as to transform them into "holy little angels." They tumble down the platforms of military parades and, suddenly, without trying, cause all the policies of good neighbors to fail. This anonymous mass, obscure and unpredictable, is slowly populating every corner of Latin America; the people of the bedbugs, the fleas, and the cockroaches, the miserable people that at this moment are gobbling down the planet. This formidable mass extends and crosses frontiers; they work as porters and mechanics, ice cream vendors (why do our countries have so much ice cream and so many sodas?), and cleaners of anything and everything, errand boys and shoe-shiners. José Agustín, a young Mexican writer, once declared that in the United States they believed: "I'm a shoe-shine boy made good." It would have been better for him to have said "a shoe-shine boy

made bad." We have all been made bad, we are all needy, all un-
wanted guests around the feast, invited at the last minute. In recog-
nizing this lies our creativity.

Translated from the Spanish by Cynthia Steele,
to whom the author dedicates this essay

A FIRE HAD TO BE LIT

ANITA
DESAI

I suppose I began to write *Fire on the Mountain* when I was eight
years old and taken to Kasauli for the summer—even if I did not put
down a word on paper then. At that time I was not the narrator of a
book, but the source of one. That summer I was suspected by my
mother of not being well or strong and requiring special attention,
and was therefore kept mostly at home which was, for the summer, a
large, square stone house on the hillside below the town. While my
brother and older sisters roamed the upper ridges in search of adven-
tures, I played by myself in the garden or wandered in the cornfields,
pine groves, and apricot orchards immediately surrounding the
house. Although I missed some grand and rather terrifying adven-
tures, I believe it was because of this imposed isolation that I absorbed my surroundings, mulled over them and retained impressions
at their most pure and vivid. I was not dissipating them by sharing
them with anyone, or diluting them by giving them only half my
attention. The flash of a silvery langur's fur through the foliage, the
odor of the dry pine needles on the hillsides, and the feel of the
stones and pieces of bark I played with in my solitary games sank

into me indelibly: they sank in so deep that I lost sight of them and forgot them.

They stirred to life again when some twenty years later I found myself living in Chandigarh (which had not existed in 1945), and going up to Kasauli for holidays once more. This time it was my children who were exploring the hillsides, and through them I relived those earlier, almost forgotten experiences of sliding down a hillside slippery with pine needles, driving away a band of langurs that had descended on our zinc roof, gazing at the smoke from a forest fire and wondering if it would draw much closer. Like seeds that had been buried deep in the soil and stirred to life on feeling a shower of rain and the coming of the right season, the memories became living experiences once again.

While walking along the Kasauli Mall I would sometimes stop by the fence to look down the steep hillside at a small village below, its haystacks and cattle and stony paths, its small population of laborers going about with their backs bent under sheaves of grass, sickles tucked in at the waist. I wondered then if it was this village—or one nearby—where an acquaintance of my mother's had been done to death, a woman I had seen perhaps half a dozen times during my childhood, and since then quite forgotten. Miss R. was a spinster lady who taught, I think, in one of the women's colleges in Delhi; she had sometimes visited my mother in order to pour out her woes to a sympathetic listener. I am afraid she met with little sympathy from me. Like my father and brother and sisters, I found her tiny desiccated figure and astonishingly loud, braying voice utterly ludicrous and would run away, choking with laughter, when I heard her voice ring out at the gate. She was afflicted with a voice no one could bear; I doubt if she had any friends. Later, she left Delhi; my mother told me she was involved in social work in a village near Kasauli. I think we received a few letters, telling of her hardships, her lack of money, her inability to do anything for the ignorant and stubborn villagers. Still later, the news came that she had been brutally assaulted and murdered by a villager, who resented her presence and her proselytizing. We were shocked. Then we forgot. She faded away.

On leaving the north and moving to Bombay, I felt the need to recapture that landscape which seemed essential to my survival—if I were not to die from the onslaught of a great and abrasive city, its unrelieved ugliness, squalor, and noise. I sat down at my desk and set myself to recreating the sounds and smells and sights of the Kasauli hills. It was my belief in the magic power of words that made me feel I could do so through an act of intense concentration—and replace my actual presence there. To do that, I had to send my eight-year-old self out into the hills again, wearing a straw hat that had slipped onto my back and chafed my shoulders, my feet in open sandals feeling the white dust and stubbing against the stones again. That child, its solitude, became the focal point of the book.

I had experienced that summer and those hills in solitude, and solitude became its natural theme. Although I had lost that sense of isolation on later holidays there, I recalled a woman who used to live on top of the hill above the cottage we rented, a Mrs. S., whom I had not known personally but knew of and whose gray melancholy presence had struck me greatly. I used to see her going for walks alone; occasionally on passing her house, I heard her playing her piano, meditatively and compellingly. I was later told of her lonely death that she seemed to have willed upon herself. She joined the small sunburnt child straying on the hillside, as the second of my two characters.

Then, I was halfway through my book, still trying to discover why these two characters—the melancholy gray lady and the cricket-like child—were where they were, when I saw a gray, indistinct figure looming over the horizon, as insubstantial as a wisp of smoke from a forest fire. For a while, I could neither recognize it nor understand its presence in my book. Then, when I began to describe it, I gave a start of astonishment as I recognized Miss R. It was her ghost that had climbed up the hillside onto the Mall and accosted me. I heard her voice ring out, shattering the silence that enclosed my two characters, in a scream for attention. In my state of shock, I forgot to laugh; in fact, I found I could not laugh any more; I saw now that she was not laughable at all, she was tragic. Although she had played a minute, indeed minuscule role in my life until then, and I had not thought about her in thirty years, she must have remained buried in my subconscious. To lay her ghost, to exorcise her unspeakable past, it was necessary to write about her. My memory of Miss R. was flawed; I saw her and remembered her from the viewpoint of a child unwilling to give her any time or sympathy—I was not capable then of either. It was therefore necessary to go back to my spare memories of her; attempt to understand and picture her wretched existence and unthinkable death—in order to arrive at what seemed to be the truth.

These characters could not exist in a vacuum; they could not float in space. They had to be provided with a background, and it had to be so real that it could be touched, heard, and felt. Kasauli provided that: sitting in a flat in Bombay and looking out over the slums smothered in city smog, I was nevertheless in touch with a different landscape, sunburnt and stark; words spun the threads that led me back to it, words were the bridge and became the web. The landscape could not possibly be just a background; it was too powerful to be merely that. Surely that twisted pine tree with two branches like outflung arms against the sky had some meaning . . . the kite floating on currents of air through the gorges and silent chasms was symbol of some mystery that I could not understand, but invited me to delve into it and discover its significance, or at least proclaim its presence.

There were other elements that went into the making of the jigsaw puzzle, some vague and others definite; the element of terror that is never absent from even the most sunlit places of childhood (Flannery O'Connor: "Anybody who has survived childhood has enough information about life to last him the rest of his days"). The research at the Pasteur Institute that I had heard about as a child was connected with the horrors of snakebite and rabies, and became very real when we later lived in a cottage that overlooked the gorge into which the Pasteur Institute emptied its chutes and from which we could see its prison-like walls and its blackened smokestacks. . . . A nighttime walk down a shadow-patterned road when we children tried to terrify each other by telling ghost stories . . . the small white graves overgrown with grass in the British cemetery. . . . Also the impression, a lasting one, made on me by Mrs. Ramsay in *To the Lighthouse* and the clinging charm of Sei Shonagon's *Pillow Book*. . . . The writing of the book became a curious mingling of the real and the remembered and the imagined—as every novel is. It is, after all, as E. M. Forster said, "won by the mind from matter" and contains elements of both. The two can be seen as locked in combat or in harmony, but the right proportions have to be found in order to balance the whole. If the book is to be strong, effective, and meaningful, then the gaps between these elements, between the real and the imagined worlds, the objective and the subjective attitudes, the extrovert and the introvert elements, have to be closed up; the two must mesh together leaving no gaps through which credulity could drain. Having built oneself such a container, it might surprise one to see, when lowering it into those depths of memory, or swinging it through the free space of imagination, what it might catch and net.

Having pinned down my butterfly with my nib, I was not finished with it; I had still to see it through the press, correct proofs, finally be faced with the sight of it in a bookshop, available to all. It had many incarnations: an English edition to begin with; then an American edition that carried the picture of a black witch on the cover; a paperback edition that displayed a bright hoopoe, a flyswatter, and a landscape that never was; then translations in which I lost sight of the original, and that became originals in themselves. . . . It was read and received reviews. I was questioned about it. Readers were disturbed: what did it all mean? Was it a real fire or a symbolic one? Why did the child start it? Did the old lady die, or faint—"or what?" Since I was responsible for it, I had to defend it. "Don't you see?" I replied. "Everyone in that book is living an illusion—their lives are built on illusions. To be rid of them, a fire had to be lit and only the child was pure enough to light it. Everything had to be burnt away in order to reduce it to ash and reveal the truth." I was surprised by my own explanation: it had not occurred to me till I gave it that it was one. Certainly it was not my intention when I began to write that book but, to my relief, it fitted; it had been fortuitous but it had turned out right—one of those instances of stumbling upon the truth rather than pursuing and capturing it.

. . .

These final and richly satisfying explanations never occur to a writer while writing the book. Such verbalizations of the conflicts, of the disappointments and pride, of satisfaction and dismay, come much later and serve chiefly to soothe one's conscience, to act as a healing, mending plaster upon a wound, to persuade one that time has not been thrown away and life not wasted. While writing one is only aware of the compulsion to write, barely understood but nevertheless powerfully felt and of which John Updike spoke when he said he wrote a particular novel "because the rhythm of my life and my 'oeuvre' demanded it, not to placate hallucinatory critical voices."

That is the very answer one might extract from a spider, if answer it could give on being asked to justify its web. It spins because spinning is what is demanded of it by the rhythm of its life, and its oeuvre.

MY VOCATION

NATALIA GINZBURG

My vocation is to write and I have known this for a long time. I hope I won't be misunderstood; I know nothing about the value of the things I am able to write. I know that writing is my vocation. When I sit down to write I feel extraordinarily at ease, and I move in an element which, it seems to me, I know extraordinarily well; I use tools that are familiar to me and they fit snugly in my hands. If I do something else, if I study a foreign language or try to learn history or geography or shorthand or if I try and speak in public or take up knitting or go on a journey, I suffer and constantly ask myself how others do these things: it always seems to me that there must be some correct way of doing these things which others know about and I don't. And it seems to me that I am deaf and blind and I feel a sort of sickness in the pit of my stomach. But when I write I never imagine that there is perhaps a better way of writing which other writers follow. I am not interested in what other writers do. But here I had better make it plain that I can only write stories. If I try to write a critical essay or an article that has been commissioned for a newspaper I don't do it very well. I have to search laboriously, as if it were outside myself, for what I am writing now. I can do it a little better than I can learn a foreign language or speak in public, but only a little better. And I always feel that I am cheating the reader with words that I have borrowed or filched from various places. I suffer and feel that I am in exile. But when I write stories I am like someone who is in her own country, walking along streets that she has known since she was a child, between walls and trees that are hers. My vocation is to write stories—invented things or things which I can remember from my own life, but in any case stories, things that are concerned only with memory and imagination and have nothing to do with erudition. This is my vocation and I shall work at it till I die. I am very happy with my vocation and I would not change it for anything in the world. I realized that it was my vocation a long time ago. Between the ages of five and ten I was still unsure, and sometimes I imagined that I would be a painter, some-times that I would ride out on horseback and conquer countries, sometimes that I would invent new machines that would be very important. But I have known since I was ten, and I worked as hard as I could at poems and novels. I still have those poems. The first poems are clumsy and they have errors of versification in them, but they are quite pleasant; and then, little by little, as time passed I wrote poems that became less and less clumsy but more and more boring and silly. However, I didn't know this and I was ashamed of the clumsy poems, while those that were silly and not so clumsy seemed to me to be very beautiful, and I used to think that one day some famous poet would discover them and have them published and write long articles about me; I imagined the words and phrases of those articles and I composed them, from beginning to end, in my head. I imag-ined that I would win the Fracchia Prize. I had heard that there was such a prize for writers. As I was unable to publish my poems in a book, since I didn't know any famous poets, I copied them neatly into an exercise book and drew a little flower on the title page and made an index and everything. It became very easy for me to write poems. I wrote about one a day. I realized that if I didn't want to write it was enough for me to read some poems by Pascoli or Gozzano or Corazzini and then I immediately wanted to. My poems came out as imitation Pascoli or imitation Gozzano or imitation Corazzini and then finally very imitation D'Annunzio when I found out that he also existed. However, I never thought that I would write poetry all my life. I wanted to write novels sooner or later. I wrote three or four during those years. There was one called *Marion or the Gipsy Girl,* another called *Molly and Dolly* (a humorous detective story), another called *A Woman* (à la D'Annunzio; in the second person; the story of a woman abandoned by her husband; I remember that there was also a cook who was a Negress), and then one that was very long and complicated with terrible stories of kidnapped girls and carriages so that I was too afraid to write it when I was alone in the house: I can remember nothing about it except that there was one phrase which pleased me very much and that tears came into my eyes as I wrote it, "He said: 'Ah! Isabella is leaving.'" The chapter finished with this phrase which was very important because it was said by the man who loved Isabella although he did not know this as he had not yet confessed it to himself. I don't remember anything about this man (I think he had a reddish beard). Isabella had long black hair with blue highlights in it; I don't know anything else about her. I know that for a long time I would feel a shiver of joy whenever I said "Ah! Isabella is leaving" to myself. I also often used to repeat a phrase which I found in a serialized novel in *Stampa* which went like this, "Murderer of Gilonne, where have you put my child?" But I was not as sure about my novels as I was about the poems. When I reread them I always discovered a weakness somewhere or other, something wrong which spoiled everything and which was impossible to change. I always used to muddle up the past and the present; I was unable to fix the story in a particular time. Parts of it were convents and carriages and a general feeling of the French Revolution, and parts of it were policemen with truncheons;

and then all of a sudden there would be a little gray housewife with a sewing machine and cats as in Carola Prosperi's novels, and this didn't go very well with the carriages and convents. I wavered between Carola Prosperi and Victor Hugo and Nick Carter's stories; I didn't really know what I wanted to do. I was also very keen on Annie Vivanti. There is a phrase in *The Devourers* when she is writing to a stranger and says to him, "I dress in brown." This was another phrase which for a long time I repeated to myself. During the day I used to murmur to myself these phrases which gave me so much pleasure—"Murderer of Gilonne," "Isabella is leaving," "I dress in brown"—and I felt immensely happy.

Writing poetry was easy. I was very pleased with my poems; to me they seemed almost perfect. I could not see what difference there was between them and real, published poems by real poets. I could not see why when I gave them to my brothers to read they laughed and said I would have done better to study Greek. I thought that perhaps my brothers didn't know much about poetry. Meanwhile I had to go to school and study Greek, Latin, mathematics, history— and I suffered a good deal and felt that I was in exile. I spent my days writing poems and copying them out in exercise books; I did not study for my lessons so I used to set the alarm for five in the morning. The alarm went off but I went on sleeping. I woke at seven, when there was no longer any time to study and I had to dress to go to school. I was not happy, I was always extremely afraid and filled with feelings of guilt and confusion. When I got to school I studied history during the Latin lesson, Greek during the history lesson, and so on, and I learnt nothing. For quite a while I thought it was all worth it because my poems were so beautiful, but at a certain moment I began to think that perhaps they were not so beautiful and it became tedious for me to write them and take the trouble to find subjects; it seemed to me that I had already dealt with every possible subject, and used all the possible words and rhymes—*speranza, lontananza; pensiero, mistero; vento, argento; fragranza, speranza* (hope, distance; thought, mystery; wind, silver; fragrance, hope). I couldn't find anything else to say. Then a very nasty period began for me, and I spent afternoons playing about with words that no longer gave me any pleasure while at the same time I felt guilty and ashamed about school. It never entered my head that I had mistaken my vocation—I wanted to write as much as ever, it was just that I could not understand why my days had suddenly become so barren and empty of words.

The first serious piece I wrote was a story, a short story of five or six pages; it came from me like a miracle in a single evening, and when afterwards I went to bed I was tired, bewildered, worn out. I had the feeling that it was a serious piece, the first that I had ever written: the poems and the novels about girls and carriages suddenly seemed very far away from me; they were the naíve and ridiculous creatures of another age and they belonged to a time that had disappeared for good. There were characters in this new story. Isabella and the man with the reddish beard were not characters; I didn't know anything about them beyond the words and phrases with which I described them—they appeared as if at random and not by my design. I had chosen the words and phrases I used for them by chance; it was as if I had a sack and had indiscriminately pulled out of it now a beard and now a cook who was a Negress or some other usable item. But this time it was not a game. This time I had invented characters with names that I could not possibly have changed; I could not have changed any part of them and I knew a great deal about them—I knew how their lives had been up to the day of my story even though I did not talk about this in the story as it was not necessary. And I knew all about the house, the bridge, the moon, and the river. I was seventeen and I had failed in Latin, Greek, and mathematics. I had cried a lot when I found out. But now that I had written the story I felt a little less ashamed. It was summer, a summer night. A window that gave on to the garden was open and dark moths fluttered about the lamp. I had written my story on squared paper and I felt happy as never before in my life; I felt I had a wealth of thoughts and words within me. The man was called Maurizio, the woman was called Anna, and the child was called Villi, and the bridge, the moon, and the river were also there. These things existed in me. And the man and the woman were neither good nor evil, but funny and a little sad and it seemed to me that I had discovered how people in books should be—funny and at the same time sad. Whichever way I looked at this story it seemed beautiful to me: there were no mistakes in it; everything happened as it should, at the right time. At that moment it seemed to me that I could write millions of stories.

And in fact I wrote quite a few, at intervals of a month or two—some were quite good and some not so good. Now I discovered that it is tiring to write something seriously. It is a bad sign if it doesn't make you tired. You cannot hope to write something serious frivolously flitting hither and thither, as it were, with one hand tied behind your back. You cannot get off so lightly. When someone writes something seriously he is lost in it, he is sucked down into it up to his eyebrows; and if there is a very strong emotion that is preoccupying him, if he is very happy or very unhappy for some let us say mundane reason which has nothing to do with the piece he is writing, then if what he is writing is real and deserves to live all those other feelings will become dormant in him. He cannot hope to keep his dear happiness or dear unhappiness whole and fresh before him; everything goes off into the distance and vanishes and he is left alone with his page. No happiness or unhappiness that is not strictly relevant to that page can exist in him; he cannot possess or belong to anything else—and if it does not happen like this, well that is a sign that the page is worthless.

And so for a certain period—which lasted about six years—I wrote short stories. Since I had discovered that characters existed it seemed to me that to *have* a character was enough to make a story. So I was always hunting for characters; I looked at the people in the tram and on the street and when I found a face that seemed suitable for a story I wove some moral details and a little anecdote around it. I also went hunting for details of dress and people's appearance, and how their houses looked inside; if I went into a new room I tried to describe it silently to myself, and I tried to find some small detail which would fit well in a story. I kept a notebook in which I wrote down some of the details I had discovered, or little similes, or episodes which I promised myself I would use in stories. For example, I would write in my notebook "She came out of the bathroom trailing the cord of her dressing-gown behind her like a long tail," "How the lavatory stinks in this house—the child said to him—When I go, I hold my breath—he added sadly," "His curls like bunches of grapes," "Red and black blankets on an unmade bed," "A pale face like a peeled potato." But I discovered how difficult it was to use these phrases when I was writing a story. The notebook became a kind of museum of phrases that were crystallized and embalmed and very difficult to use. I tried endlessly to slip the red and black blankets or the curls like bunches of grapes into a story but I never managed to. So the notebook was no help to me. I realized that in this vocation there is no such thing as "savings." If someone thinks, That's a fine detail and I don't want to waste it in the story I'm writing at the moment, I've plenty of good material here, I'll keep it in reserve for another story I'm going to write, that detail will crystallize inside him and he won't be able to use it. When someone writes a story he should throw the best of everything into it, the best of whatever he possesses and has seen, all the best things that he has accumulated throughout his life. If you carry details around inside yourself for a long time without making use of them, they wear out and waste away. Not only details but everything, all your ideas and clever notions. At the time when I was writing short stories made up of characters I had chanced on, and minute descriptive details, at that time I once saw a handcart being pushed through the street and on it was a huge mirror in a gilded frame. The greenish evening sky was reflected in it and as I stopped to watch while it went past I was feeling extremely happy, and I had the impression that something important had happened. I had been feeling very happy even before I saw the mirror, and it suddenly seemed to me that in the greenish resplendent mirror with its gilded frame the image of my own happiness was passing by me. For a long time I thought that I would put this in a story; for a long time simply remembering that handcart with the mirror on top of it made me want to write. But I was never able to include it anywhere and finally I realized that the image had died in me. Nevertheless it was very important. Because at the time when I was writing my short stories I always concentrated on gray, squalid people and things, I sought out a contemptible kind of reality lacking in glory. There was a certain malignancy in the taste I had at that time for finding minute details, an avid, mean desire for little things—little as fleas are little; I was engaged in an obstinate, scandal-mongering hunt for fleas. The mirror on the handcart seemed to offer me new possibilities, perhaps the ability to look at a more glorious and splendid kind of reality which did not require minute descriptions and cleverly noticed details but which could be conveyed in one resplendent, felicitous image.

In the last analysis I despised the characters in the short stories I was writing at that time. Since I had discovered that it works well if a character is sad and comic I made characters who, because of their comic and pitiable qualities, were so contemptible and lacking in glory that I myself could not love them. My characters always had some nervous tic or obsession or physical deformity, or some rather ridiculous bad habit—they had a broken arm in a black sling, or they had sties in their eyes, or they stuttered, or they scratched their buttocks as they talked, or they limped a little. I always had to characterize them in some such way. For me this was a method of running away from my fear that they would turn out too vague, a way of capturing their humanity (which, subconsciously, I did not believe in). Because at that time I did not realize—though when I saw the mirror on the handcart I began, confusedly, to realize it— that I was no longer dealing with characters but with puppets, quite well painted and resembling men, but puppets. When I invented them I immediately characterized them, I marked them with some grotesque detail, and there was something nasty in this; I had a kind of malign resentment against reality. It was not a resentment based on anything real, because at that time I was a happy girl, but it appeared as a kind of reaction against naïveté; it was that special resentment with which a naïve person who always thinks she is being made a fool of defends herself—the resentment of a peasant who finds himself in a city for a while and sees thieves everywhere. At first I was bold, because this seemed to me to be a great ironic triumph over the naïvely pathetic effusions which were all too ap- parent in my poems. Irony and nastiness seemed to be very impor- tant weapons in my hands; I thought they would help me write like a man, because at that time I wanted terribly to write like a man and I had a horror of anyone realizing from what I wrote that I was a woman. I almost always invented male characters because they would be the furthest and most separate from myself.

I became reasonably good at blocking out a story, at getting rid of superfluous material and introducing details and conversations at the appropriate moments. I wrote dry, clear stories that contained no blunders or mistakes of tone and that came to a convincing conclu- sion. But after a while I had had enough of this. The faces of people in the street no longer said anything interesting to me. Someone had a sty and someone had his cap on back to front and someone was wearing a scarf instead of a shirt, but these things no longer mattered to me. I was fed up with looking at things and people and describing them to myself. The world became silent for me. I could no longer find words to describe it, I no longer had any words capable of giving me pleasure. I didn't have anything anymore. I tried to re- member the mirror, but even that had died in me. I carried a burden of embalmed objects around inside of me—silent faces and ashen words, places and voices and gestures that were a dead weight on my heart, that had no flicker of life in them. And then my children were born and when they were very little I could not understand how anyone could sit herself down to write if she had children. I did not see how I could separate myself from them in order to follow some-one or other's fortunes in a story. I began to feel contempt for my vocation. Now and again I longed for it desperately and felt that I was in exile, but I tried to despise it and make fun of it and occupy myself solely with the children. I believed I had to do this. I spent my time on creamed rice and creamed barley and wondering whether there was sun or not or wind or not so that I could take the children out for a walk. The children seemed extremely important to me because they were a way of leaving my stupid stories and stupid embalmed characters behind. But I felt a ferocious longing within me and sometimes at night I almost wept when I remembered how beautiful my vocation was. I thought that I would recover it some day or other but I did not know when: I thought that I would have to wait till my children grew up and left me. Because the feeling I then had for my children was one that I had not yet learnt to control. But then little by little I learnt, and it did not even take that long. I still made tomato sauce and semolina, but simultaneously I thought about what I could be writing. At that time we were living in very beautiful countryside, in the south. I remembered my own city's streets and hills, and those streets and hills mingled with the streets and hills and meadows of the place where we were, and a new nature, something that I was once again able to love, appeared. I felt homesick for my city and in retrospect I loved it very much. I loved and understood it in a way that I had never done when I lived there, and I also loved the place where we were then living—a countryside that was white and dusty in the southern sunlight; wide meadows of scorched, bristling grass stretched away from my win-dow, and a memory of the avenues and plane-trees and high houses of my city assailed me; all this slowly took fire in me and I had a very strong desire to write. I wrote a long story, the longest I had ever written. I started writing again like someone who has never written, because it was a long time since I had written anything, and the words seemed rinsed and fresh; everything was new and, as it were, untouched, and full of taste and fragrance. I wrote in the afternoons while a local girl took my children out for a walk, and I wrote greedily and joyfully; it was a beautiful autumn and I felt very happy every day. I put a few invented people into my story and a few real people from the countryside where we were living; and some of the words that came to me as I was writing were idioms and imprecations local to that area, and which I had not known before, and these new expressions were like a yeast that fermented and gave life to all the old words. The main character was a woman, but very different from myself. Now I no longer wanted to write like a man, because I had had children and I thought I knew a great many things about tomato sauce and even if I didn't put them into my story it helped my vocation. It seemed to me that women knew things about their children that a man could never know. I wrote my story very quickly, as if I were afraid that it would run away. I called it a novel, but perhaps it was not a novel. But up till then I had always written very quickly, and always very short things, and at a certain moment I thought I realized why. Because I had brothers who were much older than me and when I was small if I talked at table they always told me to be quiet. And so I was used to speaking very fast, in a headlong fashion with the smallest possible number of words, and always afraid that the others would start talking among themselves again and stop listening to me. Perhaps this seems a rather stupid explanation; nevertheless that is how it was.

I said that the time when I was writing what I called a novel was a very happy time for me. Nothing serious had ever happened in my life; I knew nothing about sickness or betrayal or loneliness or death. Nothing in my life had ever fallen to pieces, except futile things;

nothing dear to my heart had ever been snatched away from me. I had only suffered from the listless melancholy of adolescence and the pain of not knowing how to write. And so I was happy in a fulfilled, calm way, without fear or anxiety, and with a complete faith in the stability and durability of earthly happiness. When we are happy we feel that we are cooler, clearer, more separate from reality. When we are happy we tend to create characters who are very different from ourselves; we see them in a cold, clear light as things separate from us. While our imagination and inventive energy work assertively within us we avert our eyes from our own happy, contented state and pitilessly—with a free, cruel, ironic, proud gaze—fix them on other beings. It is easy for us to invent characters, many characters, who are fundamentally different from us, and it is easy for us to construct our stories solidly—they are, as it were, well-drained and stand in a cold, clear light. What we then lack, when we are happy in this special way that has no tears or anxiety or fear in it, what we then lack is any tender, intimate sympathy with our characters and with the places and things we write about. What we lack is compassion. Superficially we are much more generous in the sense that we always find the strength to be interested in others and devote our time to them—we are not that preoccupied with ourselves because we don't need anything. But this interest of ours in others, which is so lacking in tenderness, can only get at a few relatively external aspects of their characters. The world has only one dimension for us and lacks secrets and shadows; we are able to guess at and create the sadness we have not experienced by virtue of the imaginative strength within us, but we always see it in a sterile, frozen light as something that does not concern us and that has no roots within us.

Our personal happiness or unhappiness, our *terrestrial* condition, has a great importance for the things we write. I said before that at the moment someone is writing he is miraculously driven to forget the immediate circumstances of his own life. This is certainly true. But whether we are happy or unhappy leads us to write in one way or another. When we are happy our imagination is stronger; when we are unhappy our memory works with greater vitality. Suffering makes the imagination weak and lazy; it moves, but unwillingly and heavily, with the weak movements of someone who is ill, with the weariness and caution of sick, feverish limbs; it is difficult for us to turn our eyes away from our own life and our own state, from the thirst and restlessness that pervade us. And so memories of our own past constantly crop up in the things we write; our own voice constantly echoes there and we are unable to silence it. A particular sympathy grows up between us and the characters that we invent—a sympathy that is tender and almost maternal, warm and damp with tears, intimately physical and stifling. We are deeply, painfully rooted in every being and thing in the world, the world which has become filled with echoes and trembling and shadows, to which we are bound by a devout and passionate pity. Then we risk foundering on a dark lake of stagnant, dead water, and dragging our mind's creations down with us, so that they are left to perish among dead rats and rotting flowers in a dark, warm whirlpool. As far as the things we write are concerned, there is a danger in grief just as there is a danger in happiness. Because poetic beauty is a mixture of ruthlessness, pride, irony, physical tenderness, of imagination and memory, of clarity and obscurity—and if we cannot gather all things together we are left with something meager, unreliable, and hardly alive.

And you have to realize that you cannot hope to console yourself for your grief by writing. You cannot deceive yourself by hoping for caresses and lullabies from your vocation. In my life there have been interminable, desolate, empty Sundays in which I desperately wanted to write something that would console me for my loneliness and boredom, so that I could be calmed and soothed by phrases and words. But I could not write a single line. My vocation has always rejected me; it does not want to know about me. Because this vocation is never a consolation or a way of passing the time. It is not a companion. This vocation is a master who is able to beat us till the blood flows, a master who reviles and condemns us. We must swallow our saliva and our tears and grit our teeth and dry the blood from our wounds and serve him. Serve him when he asks. Then he will help us up onto our feet, fix our feet firmly on the ground; he will help us overcome madness and delirium, fever and despair. But he has to be the one who gives the orders and he always refuses to pay attention to us when we need him.

After the time when I lived in the south I got to know grief very well—a real, irremediable and incurable grief that shattered my life, and when I tried to put it together again I realized that I and my life had become something irreconcilable with what had gone before. Only my vocation remained unchanged, but it is profoundly misleading to say that even that was unchanged—the tools were still the same but the way I used them had altered. At first I hated it, it disgusted me, but I knew very well that I would end up returning to it, and that it would save me. Sometimes I would think that I had not been so unfortunate in my life and that I was unjust when I accused destiny of never having shown me any kindness, because it had given me my three children and my vocation. Besides, I could not imagine my life without my vocation. It was always there, it had never left me for a moment, and when I believed that it slept its vigilant, shining eyes were still watching me.

Such is my vocation. It does not produce much money and it is always necessary to follow some other vocation simultaneously in order to live. Though sometimes it produces a little, and it is very satisfying to have money because of it—it is like receiving money and presents from the hands of someone you love. Such is my vocation. I do not, I repeat, know much about the value of the results it has given me or could give me; or it would be better to say that I know the relative though certainly not the absolute value of the results I have already obtained. When I write something I usually think it is very important and that I am a very fine writer. I think this happens to everyone. But there is one corner of my mind in which I know very well what I am, which is a small, a very small writer. I swear I know it. But that doesn't matter much to me. Only I don't want to think about names: I can see that if I am asked "A small writer like who?" it would sadden me to think of the names of other small writers. I prefer to think that no one has ever been like me, however small, however much a mosquito or a flea of a writer I may be. The important thing is to be convinced that this really is your vocation, your profession, something you will do all your life. But as a vocation it is no joke. There are innumerable dangers besides those I have mentioned. We are constantly threatened with grave dangers whenever we write a page. There is the danger of suddenly starting to be flirtatious and of singing. I always have a crazy desire to sing and I have to be very careful that I don't. And there is the danger of cheating with words that do not really exist within us, that we have picked up by chance from outside of ourselves and which we skillfully slip in because we have become a bit dishonest. There is the danger of cheating and being dishonest. As you see, it is quite a difficult vocation, but it is the finest one in the world. The days and houses of our lives, the days and houses of the people with whom we are involved, books and images and thoughts and conversations—all these things feed it, and it grows within us. It is a vocation which also feeds on terrible things; it swallows the best and the worst in our lives and our evil feelings flow in its blood just as much as our benevolent feelings. It feeds itself, and grows within us.

This essay is reprinted from the author's collection
The Little Virtues, *translated from the Italian by Dick Davis*

SHIFTING THINGS

JOY
WILLIAMS

My father is a Congregational minister. My grandfather was a minister. My family is Welsh. I grew up, an only child, in Maine. This is not a paragraph from one of my stories. It is a paragraph from my life. My real life.

I was fascinated by the words in the Bible, and the stories. The stories aren't comforting or sentimental, they're tremendous and ruthless, and the words—*horses* and *fish, blind men* and *dead men*—all those words meant something other than what they appeared to mean, they were all representations of other things, things I could and couldn't imagine. Water wasn't water, seeds weren't seeds. This thrilled me. Everything, as image, was totally something else. There were levels of meanings in images, in sentences, in stories.

·   ·   ·

I wanted to write.

·   ·   ·

The year I went to college I received *three* copies of Marguerite Young's *Miss MacIntosh, My Darling* for Christmas. It was as though my loved ones were saying—So you want to be a writer! Well, it took this woman seventeen years to write this book which is about the search for reality in a world of illusion and nightmare. It's pretty much unreadable but it's supposed to be a work of art. We guess this is how it's done and it's by a woman too so . . . good luck.

· · ·

I wrote to Flannery O'Connor's mother once. I said I really liked her daughter's stories and could I have a picture of her. Meaning her daughter, of course. She wrote back and said I sure could not.

· · ·

At the time I didn't realize what it was, the true nature of the peculiar gift the writer gives the reader.

· · ·

I like the short story as a form. The intensity of it, the swiftness. Assemble the ambulances. Something is going to happen.

· · ·

More can probably be found out about a writer from a single paragraph of work than from any interview or essay. Gertrude Stein said that paragraphs are emotional whereas sentences are not. She also said that the American way of writing was the disembodied way of disconnecting something from anything and anything from something. She suggested that something was always floating above the American paragraph—the well-done American paragraph—something detached from what it said and what it did.

· · ·

Here is a paragraph of mine. *Turnupseed lived on the mainland in a little cement block house on land sucked senseless by the phosphate interests. Every time he tried to plant a tree in the queer, floppy soil, it perished.* What does that tell you about me? It tells you that I sometimes find safety in the comic, because really there is a pit, a panic beneath everything and the comic is a safety net there to keep from falling further. It swings there kindly and yet it should be removed, really. Don't count on the net. Fall further.

. . .

I write out of a sense of guilt. I believe in guilt. There's not enough guilt around these days for my taste.

. . .

A woman recently told me that after reading my first novel, *State of Grace,* she kept dreaming that her house was burning down. I was charmed by this of course. At the same time, I suspected it had been said before about someone else. Words, you know. They're around. They've been used a lot.

. . .

I don't dream much. I know this is not a good signifier. Writers are supposed to dream and keep diaries. Women writers are supposed to, that is. Men don't have to necessarily. I frequently have nightmares. They take two inarticulatable forms. There are no images in them at all. They are pure fear and dismay, a sense of the tremendous strength of the dark, a sense that I have not done what it was I knew I should have done.

. . .

What I can conjure up in the daylight hours when I close my eyes tight are the faces of people. They are all totally unique, people I have never seen before or written about, blooming and fading one after another behind my shut lids. I don't understand it. They come in the bright Florida sunlight. I would prefer them to be in the shape of animals . . . *other* things. But they are the faces of people. Strangers, very clear, but without their stories.

. . .

The writer has to maintain a curious disassociation with the world. The act of writing in itself is a highly self-conscious retreat from the world. I live in beautiful places but I have to stay cooped up in a small, almost dark room if I'm ever going to get anything done. And I have to stay there for hours and hours, day after day, making this *thing,* setting this created, unreal thing in motion, a story. The literal isn't interesting, but the literal must be perfectly, surprisingly rendered because the search is always to see things in a new way. That is essential.

. . .

And then it just seems preposterous. There I am, choosing my words so carefully, trying to build this pure, unanalyzable, transparent, honest thing in this dim room with the shades drawn and out there is the world, indecent, cruel, apathetic, a world where the seas are being trashed, the desert bladed, the wolves shot, the eagles poisoned, where people show up at planning and zoning meetings waving signs that say *My Family Can't Eat the Environment.* That sentence is ill, it is a virus of a sentence, and as a writer, I should be able to defeat it and its defenders handily. With the perfect words, I should be able to point out, reasonably, that in fact the individual's family *is* eating the environment, that they are consuming it with sprawl and greed and materialistic hungers and turning it into—shit. But perfect words fail me. I don't want my words. I want to throttle this person, beat him over the head with his stupid sign.

. . .

I think what happens to many writers is that they reach a certain age and they look around and think, My God, what an indulgence this writing is—stories! I mean, really—and then they go out and involve themselves in a more active way with the world. Writers must never engage the world in their stories. The writer must write stories. Or get out in the world and beat people over the head with their stupid signs.

. . .

Oh thou lord of life, send my roots rain, Hopkins wrote. Some writers write too much. The rain doesn't come, but they write still. And they are wilting while pretending they are a tree in bloom. Sometimes the literary establishment encourages them in this belief.

. . .

I was once at lunch with a well-known writer and his family. It was our first meeting. Other people were there as well. It was a beautiful winter day in Key West. There I was, being friendly, drinking my eleven martinis or what have you, hair brushed as well as possible, napkin in lap, nibbling and chatting away, only to have the well-known writer remark later—"I expected her to be more twisted."

. . .

Jean Rhys once said that to be a writer you have to be a demon or a fraud. I don't feel myself to be particularly demonic and in person I am an absolute fraud. Everything rests on the awareness that a hidden life exists.

. . .

There's a lot of flash in the story form these days. A lot of dazzle and dependence upon the net. Houdini said that of all his tricks the most difficult to perform was the wet sheet escape. The wet sheet treatment was used in lunatic asylums to restrain violent patients. It was very difficult to escape from being bound in a wet sheet. But this escape was not popular with the audiences. They wanted him to escape from chains and dead whales and water-filled safes. These things were easier to do than they appeared. A lot of fiction is stagey now—the equivalent of making an elephant disappear—*right before your eyes.* It's easy to make an elephant disappear. The farmers of Zimbabwe are doing it every day.

. . .

The equivalent of the wet sheet escape in fiction, perhaps, would be to create a character who gets out of life having lived it, having truly spectacularly lived it, used it all up. This would have to be done with words of course.

. . .

The surface of the good story is severely simple. Clean and treacherous as new ice. Below the surface is accident, chaos, uncertainty—beautiful, shifting things. I believe in the mystery of things, their spiritual rhythm. I am not interested in man-woman things much. In-out. Or love. I am interested in loneliness, obsession, desperation. Well, perhaps I am interested in love. I am not interested in woman-woman matters much. Feminist matters. Support and consolation matters. Transformation is what I'm interested in the most. What it is that is beyond and beneath things. Moments, the levels in moments.

. . .

None of this is what I long to say. I long to say other things. I write stories in my attempt to say them.

DIPT ME IN INK

ELIZABETH
JOLLEY

. . . what sin to me unknown dipt me in ink . . .

I always thought I came from a family of no consequence but
looking back I remember that when I was about eight years old my
father invented heat and light. He wrote two textbooks for school
children. The one on heat had a red cover and the one on light was
blue. As for inheritance, what fool would claim, ticking the appropriate boxes on the application form for an exclusive school of
nursing, a grandpa who died of blood poisoning following severe
scalding from the freshly boiled kettle he was carrying when he fell
in his last epileptic fit. Then there was the other grandpa who must
have owned a disease which, though not acute for himself, destroyed
my mother's mother and subsequently three stepmothers. (My
mother grew up in a convent.) Aunt Maud and a mysterious cousin
called Dorothy were talked about in whispers. Both were said to be
mad. Who would acknowledge—with irresponsible ticks—the
grandfathers, the aunt, and the cousin?

The wartime St. Thomas's Hospital, evacuated to smaller hospitals in Surrey, was originally the place where Florence Nightingale

made nursing into a profession for ladies. Ladies abounded. One of the probationers (the name for student nurses then) was the daughter of a member of the British War Cabinet. She never had any of the regulation black woolen stockings and was adept at borrowing. But the application form. In addition to the confessions about disease and mental health, the question was asked: *How many maids does your mother keep?* Recalling my mother bent over the sink or the gas boiler I conjured images of devout women with peaceful honest faces, capable hands, and comforting bosoms and I wrote *two* on the form and was accepted. Sometimes I think lovingly of these two maids, dressing them in neat black dresses and the traditional spotless white caps and aprons. One of them, devoted to me and fond of sewing, filled my wardrobe which in truth had nothing in it except my school winter coat, a garment of such sterling quality that it accompanied me, belonging to no fashion, during all the years of the war and longer.

What kind of marriage can spring from the moving sight of Goethe's Werther first observing the youthful and charming Lotte distributing slices of bread at dusk to the small children in her care? My father first beheld my mother in a similar pose but in very different circumstances. She was sharing out soup and bread between her near starving pupils in a school in Vienna. A deeply moving scene but not a good guide to marriage. My father was in Vienna as a relief worker with the Quakers immediately after the First World War. He was distributing food and clothes.

Clytemnestra tells Electra that a daughter can never know and understand the previous experience of the mother.

> . . . I agree, one should not speak
> Bitterly. But when people judge someone,
> they ought
> To learn the facts, and then hate, if they've
> reason to

And if they find no reason, then they should
not hate.

When I was twelve my mother gave me a little needlebook she
had made. Perhaps she hoped the loving verse embroidered on the
cover would express her tenderness in some way. I still have the
book and perhaps I understand now, too late, something of her hopes
and of her suffering.

If I have always been on the edge, something of an exile—
not being a Birth Right Quaker at a Quaker boarding school;
being a nurse in training alongside girls from *good* families, that is,
county families where twin sets and pearls were not just a joke; later
in life being a newcomer to Australia where, though the language
is the same, the climate and customs are very different—this comes
in part, too, from an earlier sense of being on the edge and the
feeling of exile experienced by my mother and father. Perhaps my
experience of homesickness and exile starts, without any knowledge
or understanding, from early memories of incomprehensible unhappiness.

At the age of eleven I was sent to boarding school. Unaccustomed
to being with other children and missing the Midlands smell of the
bone and glue factory and the heave and roar of the blast furnaces, I
cried. Between autumn-berried hedgerows I cried in the middle of a
road which seemed to be leading nowhere. I began to write stories at
school, perhaps to overcome the pain of homesickness. Homesickness
seems to be bitter and wasteful but, of course, all experience, in the
end, is useful, especially for the writer.

Is there any way in which a writer can see herself from outside?
Probably not. The nearest approach is to try and see how she has
become what she is:

Why did I write? What sin to me unknown
Dipt me in ink, my parents or my own?

It would seem that all writers draw heavily on their early experience but in different ways. Some directly but perhaps some more indirectly. One thinks of Tolstoy, Wordsworth, Traherne. The experience may be happy or unhappy. Which it is does not alter its influence. It might be thought that Gorky and Dickens might have obliterated all memory of their childhoods!

My mother and father were married in Vienna soon after the Great War which ended in defeat and destruction of the Habsburg Empire. Vienna was no longer the administrative center of a large empire. My mother's father (the grandpa who had four wives) had been a general in the Imperial Army; he belonged to the great number of people whose reason for existence disappeared with the emperor.

My father with his fine white teeth and thick hair suggested, in his appearance, a life in England which would restore prosperity and social status. My mother confessed later to imagining that she would live in a large country house set in its own park. The England of her hopes did not turn out to be as expected. My father was a teacher in the heart of England's Industrial Midlands, the Black Country, an area of coal mines, brickworks, iron and steel foundries, factories, and rows of mean little houses in narrow streets.

Because of her marriage my mother was an exile. I remember that her homesickness lasted throughout her life. It was a longing for a homeland as it had been and not for what it had become.

My father loved my mother very much and always spoke German at home. German was the language of the household even though my mother spoke English fluently—with a Viennese accent and intonation. At the age of six when I started school, surrendering to my surroundings, I stopped speaking German.

My father's exile came about because of his ideals. During the Great War he suffered brutal imprisonment as a conscientious objector. His father (the grandfather who scalded himself) disowned him, turning him out of the house in front of the gathered neighbors, because of his beliefs and the disgrace of being in prison. He returned from Vienna bringing a wife, an impoverished aristocrat, to his father's house from an enemy country. When speaking about this later he was not bitter about his father but he did say that he felt for many years, because of the experience, that he had been "warped." He said, too, that one of the things about being in prison was that there was no grass and there were no flowers. He was never able to face cocoa or porridge because of the time in prison. Though, with his face averted, he made both for us when we were children. It was as if he were trying to offer an apology when he talked shyly of those times. He wept during the declaration of the Second World War because he could not believe that the same kind of cruelties would be carried out all over again. One of the things which had shocked him in 1914 was the excitement and eager anticipation for "bloodshed" among the people crowding the streets. It was as if they needed this excitement, as if their ordinary lives were too dull. In 1939 he stood on street corners giving away copies of *Peace News*. He said it was sad that people needed a war to make them feel neighborly; drawn together because it was a time of disaster. I went unwillingly and handed out *Peace News*. I am glad now that I stood with him and I have since been deeply ashamed of my unwillingness. I was brought up at home and at school to feel that all war is wrong.

My novel *Milk and Honey* contains the shadows and the weeping of people my mother and father tried to help before and during the second war. Many refugees came to our house and often my sister and I slept on the sofa or the floor because there were people who needed our beds.

During my childhood we lived in a neighborhood curious about and hostile to foreigners. My father, containing in himself conflicts between science (his subject), human effort, and what is called religion, took us away from school when I was eight. In spite of being a teacher he thought school spoiled childhood innocence. We had lessons at home with a series of French and Austrian governesses.

Perhaps the wireless lessons were the most successful. Images sprang from the quality and the tone of voice whether the voice was describing the affairs of Parliament, the dangers of unwashed clothes and milk jugs, the circulation of the blood, or the plight of the *Flying Dutchman*. Because we did not go to school and because German was spoken at home we were exiles in our own street. We retreated into fantasy. Our childhood was one long game of people. We were each other's nephews. "I'm her nephew," I told the postmistress, "and she's my nephew." With sofa cushions on our heads we said we were widows. The date-box buses we pushed round on the linoleum stopped at the table legs to pick up the waiting passengers, the little china pigs and dogs and cats, brought by relatives who travelled, and an assortment of wooden clothes pegs hand-painted to look like sailors and Spanish dancers.

Then there were the dolls' houses side by side, opened so that the rooms and lives within were all revealed. In the magic of these openings, the game was an endless story of our own composing from one day to the next for years . . .

I am not attempting a self-analysis. The household which presented itself to me as both strange and normal encouraged me to observe. My mother was given to moods. Storms blew up unexpectedly, were savage, and disappeared again as quickly. The governesses departed abruptly, in tears, leaning on my father's arm as he escorted them in turn to the railway station. I became by nature and circumstance a placator and learned to read every change in the eye, every crease in the brow. I am still a placator. Other people's households, if I am a guest, inadvertently trouble me and in my own house I am not able to work if there is some problem or unhappiness which needs sorting out or comforting. The best time for me to write is when other people are asleep. I am not needed in their dreams. I have developed the habit of writing for some hours during the night, working from the quick notes made during the day.

I cannot explain why I am a fiction writer unless the explanation comes in part from a response to my experience of the world in which I grew up and to the strange new world in which we exist today. I do not maintain that a writer should conceal her private life. What must come first are the words, which must not be twisted to fit some preconceived image of the writer. Sometimes what is most important after infancy is the experience which finds expression only in writing. It is the word which is not spoken, the resolve which is not kept, which become a part of the created. It is as if these things emerge from hidden pathways in an unexpected form. Writing fiction is not easy for me; to write facts is almost impossible.

There is an excitement in exploring characters and in seeing how they react with each other in different situations. I have always kept diaries and journals ever since I was a child. Lately I have noticed that I do not want to write in the journal because of a feeling that I am encouraging sad thoughts and increasing anxiety by dwelling at length on troublesome things and writing about them. I prefer now to retain the ability to make the quick note of truth and awareness, to notice some small thing about a person, a stranger—perhaps someone choosing knitting wool in the supermarket, something like that—and move into imaginative fiction from the small truthful moment, the little picture, the idea which is so slender it hardly seems to matter. And then suddenly I am exploring human feelings and reasons.

I do not think I lack social awareness. When I look back at my earlier writing, I find themes which were then mostly avoided but are now widely discussed. Imaginative writing can increase awareness but it cannot demonstrate the need for specific programs. When I write "I" in a story or a novel I do not mean I—myself. Some people have been disappointed that I am not any one or all of my characters.

Sometimes a childhood memory becomes suddenly vivid and powerful without it being written down. One of these was a game which my father described one evening when he was making our cocoa. I suppose I must have been about five or six years old. I liked to hear things about him. He and his sister (my aunt) played a game called horses and carts, he told us; they played on the kitchen table with an assortment of screws and nails and small nuts and bolts. The table was the street and the nuts and bolts and things went up and down, to and fro, fast and slow on the table; they were the horses and carts and that is how they played. In between games the screws and nails and things were kept in a jar with a screw-top lid.

More than fifty years later, having the sound still in my head, I gave the game to a character:

> We're running still, lightly now, one foot—two foot—one foot—two foot—foot—foot—foot—breathe in breathe out breathe in. Side by side we're running, easily.
>
> "What about the kitchen table?" he asks me. "Where did yer put yer nuts and bolts?" His breathing's easier. "Where'd you put yer horses and carts of a night time?"
>
> "I knew you'd ask that," I say. "I'll tell you. My dad made me a bit of a table out of an old box in the trailer and every night I set out my horses and carts, dot—dot—dotty—dot—up and down, to and fro along the road, fast and slow, my horses and carts passed each other, stopped to let each other go by, they turned into the roadway and sometimes they collided."

The boy's game as he plays it while his father looks on parallels some of the action in the story.

The strange thing is that my sister, who is about a year younger than I am, does not remember my father describing the horses and carts game.

In my childhood there were enrichments which at the time did not seem particularly enriching. People played the piano and sang Schubert *Lieder*. My father sat with one hand shading his eyes but I saw his tears. Then the music changed and someone sang *How do you feel when you marry your ideal Ever so goosey goosey goosey.* And someone else sang "The Wedding of the Painted Doll." My mother danced twirling her beads, strings of them; she danced kicking her feet out to the sides, heels up, toes down and turned in. Across the room she danced, across the room and back. How can it be explained that these pictures of those times and the songs which I never thought about for years came back to me to be a part of a short story?

Music is important to me. Certain passages of music, whenever I hear them, recreate certain characters. I seem to see the characters again and again as I once saw them when first writing about them. It seems that music helps me to show greater depths in the creating of the characters through the effect music has on them. Daphne in the novel *The Sugar Mother* plays an ancient record of the Indian love call from *Hiawatha* in the bathroom before a scene which she intends to be erotic. Edwin Page, in the same novel, remembers a Mozart piano concerto which suggests to him a fault in the music which is there on purpose and is put right. He says he can hear the going back over the notes and then the going forward in correction. To him this suggests that there can be a fault in life which can be put right in the same manner, but Daphne points out that this is not so. The music does not go back to allow for correction but presses on in the way it was going. A parallel for events in Edwin's life? Edwin is the hopeful dreamer and Daphne is seen to be the outspoken realist.

My character Miss Hailey, in the novel *Mr. Scobie's Riddle,* grew from the sight of a woman in an unusual straw hat. That was all I noticed about her when passing her in the street. When I made a note about the hat, at home, I imagined how pleased the woman in the hat (Miss Hailey) would be to be able to tell someone the way. Later when I discovered that Miss Hailey had the horns from *Eroica* stored within her I began to know more and more about her.

Hester Harper in the novel *The Well* is aware that while she listens to Mozart she changes from being the severe woman she is by reputation:

> She knew from listening alone that while she listened her mouth took on a different shape, the lips drawn together and pursed . . . she understood the possibility that her whole body was, during the music, different. Without meaning to she knew it was not only her lips; it was all the seriousness and tenderness which entered and set the bones of her jaw and changed the movement of her eyebrows and the tilt of her head . . .

I do not know if this is an interesting fact but I am the sort of person who needs to create a superficial order in my surroundings before I can confront the confusion which exists in my mind and in the scattered notes I gather over days, weeks, months, and years for the making of a story or a novel. I have to know in advance what I am going to prepare for the family dinner. I like to have the essentials of housework done and correspondence answered before working at the novel—if I am going to work during the day. I find it very hard to emerge from the fiction to an uncared-for house. The move from the desk to the domestic, toward the end of an afternoon, is one of the most painful experiences. I do not think this is hard for women only, but perhaps women more often find themselves in this position even in these times when women are "liberated"—and in spite of the washing machine and the dishwasher.

I never write a synopsis or an outline. If I did I might lose the idea before it was born. The language of the synopsis might kill the energy and rhythm of the special writing needed for the story. I often wish that in writing I could start with the first words and move smoothly on and on to the last words. Writing for me is a ragged and restless activity with scattered fragments to be pieced together rather like a patchwork quilt. I rewrite a great deal and usually write the first pages last and often put off writing the end for a long time. I cannot explain any of this.

I came to Western Australia from Britain in the middle of my life. I realize that the freshness of my observation can distort as well as illuminate. The impact of the new country does not obliterate the previous one but sharpens memory, thought, and feeling thus providing a contrasting theme or setting. There are advantages in having several landscapes. In the novel *Miss Peabody's Inheritance* I make use of several backgrounds—Britain, Europe, and Western Australia. Conveniently there can be details of journeys and places visited en route. The landscape of my writing is not to be found clearly on any map. The light and shade of a particular tree or the effect of water on a paddock at a particular moment may be used. In the story "Two Men Running" one of the men, longing for his destroyed life to become whole again, talks to his companion about aspects of his life and an awareness which he usually keeps hidden:

> "The gravel pits, the hills, the catchment and the foxgloves in the catchment. Did you know," I ask him. "Did you know that where water collects and runs off the rocks there are different flowers growing there? Did you know that because of this water, a paddock can be deep purple like a plum? And then, if you think about plums, the different colours range from deep purple through to the pale pearly green of the translucent satsuma before it ripens. Because of water that's how a paddock can look from one end to the other. It's the same with people ..."

In writing the above I was trying to show something of my character's need to re-create the wholesomeness of the landscape of his childhood. A consolation in his time of trouble.

It used to be the fashion, or perhaps there was a need, for Western Australian writers to deny their region. Some years ago an editor told me that I was *revealing* the Western Australian setting in a novel by putting in jarrah trees and the fact that looking westward it was possible to see the sea. The editor's geography was not foolproof, for there are other places in Australia from which the sea can be seen westward. I kept the offending details in the novel. Characters and themes are often universal and the landscape and setting from the writer's own region can bring to the work a particular flavor. In Western Australia, in the vastness of this one-third of the whole continent, there are a variety of regions. Travelling inland in an easterly direction from the seashore there are the suburbs, the city, the sand plains, and the wide valley of the Swan River where the vineyards lie in neat patterns, a well-made patchwork. Then there are the escarpment, bush and semi-rural land, more bush—partly cleared for horses and sheep—and then the wheat country for miles to the rabbitproof fence beyond which lies one of the great deserts.

For some years I have been teaching in the English Department at Curtin University of Technology, Perth. I teach, too, in the prisons and in the remote country districts. I think that teaching, like nursing, helps writing. Certainly working with people does not hamper the writer. I often make long journeys alone by car to remote wheat towns and farms. Sometimes during these long drives I stop the car and walk for a while at the side of the long straight road, low down between the paddocks which stretch endlessly on both sides of faraway horizons. A practical consideration which brought me into a new perspective was the realization that nowadays a tiny handful of unseen people produce from the vast landscape enormous quantities of food. I find that I like to feel small and insignificant on one of these empty roads with the great dome of the familiar sky above, a floating roof of light clear air. I have given Hester Harper in the novel *The Well* this same experience and feeling, though I am not Hester and my life has never been like hers.

The landscape can be used to parallel the attitudes and feelings of my characters. At the beginning of the novel *Foxybaby,* Miss Porch sets off on a long lonely drive to a distant and remote place where she is to be a drama tutor in a summer school:

> There is only one road going east from the township of Cheathem West and this road after approximately two hours of sedate driving (one hour for the reckless) becomes the main high street of Cheathem East.
>
> There are scarcely any houses in Cheathem East as very few people live there. There is no hotel and no shop.
>
> Scattered between the two Cheathems are a few lonely farms tucked and folded as if sewn neatly into the landscape for many years. In places, where the road rises, the dark seams of these farms can be seen in the distance. It is as if they are embroidered with rich green wool or silk on a golden background. In the design of the embroidery are a few trees and some silent houses and sheds. Narrow places, fenced off and watered sparingly, produce a little more of the dark-green effect in the picture.
>
> At intervals, sometimes as if they do not belong to anyone in particular, there are unsupervised windmills turning and clicking with a kind of solemn and honest obedience.

Miss Porch journeys all day toward her last hour of driving through a landscape which seems to be without people. I was able to use the silence of this landscape as a contrast to the bizarre crowd of noisy people she encounters at the school.

Western Australian writers no longer hide their region. The climate of acceptance has changed dramatically in Australia during the last decade. Contemporary fiction and poetry are able to reflect with accuracy the landscape and the society in which the writer lives. There is an audience now for the strong voices from a greater number of women writers.

Over the years it has become clear to me that I am deeply interested in people. I am curious about their motives, their feelings, their ambitions, and their hopes and disappointments. It seems to me that every person is a kind of miracle in both the anatomy and the physiology. A miracle, too, in the use of the mind, the intelligence, the memory, and the emotions—unbelievably miraculous. To study and to write about the manifestation of human life, to create characters and situations from the observation of real life is a great privilege. In spite of the excitement and the sense of privilege, writing is, for me, an act of the will.

I want, in my writing, to be optimistic and fond.

The fiction writer has the opportunity to offer people something entertaining but, at the same time, might be able to change a person's outlook on life or their direction, perhaps toward the more loving and optimistic—in spite of the often grim vision of the writer. All sides of human life can be looked upon.

I think people need cherishing. Perhaps the ability to cherish and to feel cherished in adult life comes, in part, from the forgotten experience of the cherishing, the love and the hopes, poured upon the child by the mother and the father, the grandmother and grandfather.

In the novel *Tess of the D'Urbervilles* Hardy describes the Durbeyfield children as being passengers in the Durbeyfield ship, depending on their parents for everything:

> If the heads of the Durbeyfield household chose to sail into difficulty, disaster, starvation, disease, degradation, death, thither were these half-dozen little captives under hatches compelled to sail with them . . .

Because of being under the hatches of my father's beliefs, his ideals and his innocence, I have had certain experiences which might be thought to be unusual. One of these was my being in Germany at a time when people, without my father's optimism, would not have considered being in that country. I was in a German schoolgirls' camp about fifteen miles from Hamburg during the summer of 1939. The summer camp ended abruptly for me when I was rushed in an unreliable car to the docks and pushed onto a small ship, a cargo boat bound for Hull. I lay on the deck, seasick and surrounded by baskets and baskets of bilberries. As it turned out, it was the last boat to leave for Britain. Had I not made the bilberry basket journey just then, my life might have been very different.

I have never considered this before, but I think I alternate between optimism and anxiety. I realize that should either of these get out of hand I would probably need a clever doctor. This writing about myself and my work, this self-examination disturbs me. I would prefer to be trying to write fiction.

The best thing about writing books, for me, is when a stranger comes up to me in the supermarket and tells me about one of the books and how it was either disliked or liked. Sometimes the book being described is only partly one of mine and mostly someone else's. But that doesn't really matter . . .

ASPIRADORA

DIANE
JOHNSON

As women we are taught not to speak of ourselves, but of the other person, asking him "What do you do? Tell me about your work." One's own work becomes almost a secret and antisocial pursuit, a hobby or eccentricity, like button collecting, or dypsomania. At least it has taken me some years to learn to speak of my own work, especially in a magisterial tone, as something that might be of interest to others.

The subject here I take to be: how I do my work, and how I think about it. But the odd thing is that because I am not used to speaking of it, I'm not used to thinking about it either. The time I have for it, I spend doing it. What I think about is the work at hand, the novel or essay, trying to get the thoughts right, putting the events in the right order, and the names of the characters. In other words, a writing day is so filled with practical decisions that one tends to lose sight of, or never to have glimpsed, "My Work" in the overall sense—the things that characterize it, and distinguish it from the work of other people.

I am always interested, though, to read critics who have views on my typical themes or techniques, and I can usually see what they mean, one exception being violence. I know that critics often think of me as being preoccupied with violence, whereas to me it seems I never think of it at all. In the books there are violent episodes, no doubt about it. But I think of these as being reflections of life in our society—social realism, not my psyche in particular.

How I think about my work is indistinguishable from the way I think about my needlepoint or cooking: here is the project I'm involved in. It is play. In this sense, all my life is spent in play—sewing or needlepoint, or picking flowers, or writing, or buying groceries. Being a housewife and mother, I have duties, too, but I am apt to shirk duty or wander off in the middle of it, so I can't really claim to have sacrificed my writing to my housework, the way it seems to some women that they have done.

I tend to get interested in technical or formal problems in novel-writing, and I think each of my books reflects a slightly different preoccupation, which makes each differ from the last. I think that to set oneself new problems is the only way to grow as a writer; but I know that readers, on the other hand, tend to wish you would do the same things over (until you get them right, anyhow). I suppose, at first, a writer's preoccupation tends to be with point of view, since you quickly learn that this is the most crucial and difficult choice you as the author have to make. My first novel, *Fair Game*—which is totally out of print, I hardly have any copies myself, and it has been years since I looked at it—was written from the points of view of several male characters who were all in love with one female character, Dabney. Looking back on it, I find it strange that I would try to write from a male point of view, let alone three or four, and even stranger that I should have avoided the consciousness of the woman character. In a way this was part of the novel's design—the point being that none of them understood her and only saw her as the mirror of their desires, each differently. But now I wonder, too, whether I wasn't influenced (this was around 1965) by all the traditional novels I had read, which usually have male narrators, and hence found the male voice easier to emulate. Growing up, I didn't like girl's novels—hated *Little Women.* I liked sea stories, of pirates and adventure. At that period female narrators tended to be mad, or desperately subjective, full of love or fear or some other emotion, and not employed for the purpose of rendering objective and reliable accounts of the world.

I became aware of this tradition of the unreliable female narrator when writing *The Shadow Knows,* or rather when reading the reviews of it. At that time, I was interested in the detective genre, at least in its smart, French incarnations, and the design of *Shadow* shows this—there's a detective ("the famous inspector") and a suspense situation. Someone is trying to murder the heroine, there are suspects and so on. It seemed to me that the metaphorical possibilities of detective stories for getting at issues of urban fear, guilt, and race relations in American society are enormous, and these were for me the subject of this novel. These were serious preoccupations for me, so of course I was quite surprised to read a number of critics who understood the novel as being about paranoia, a woman close to madness, the thinness of the line between madness and sanity and so on. In other words, many readers were not able to believe objective descriptions of events ("someone has put a dead cat on my doorstep") because (I suppose) the narrator was a woman.

Thinking about this later, I have come to see that the fact that the woman was young and, as people say nowadays, sexually active made people believe her less—the problem that rape victims have. An elderly grandmother can be used as a reliable narrator. But I also have to admit, speaking again of the critical reception of *The Shadow Knows,* that critics often see things in a novel that the writer wasn't conscious of putting in, and often one can see that the critics are right. In this case, though, I never have quite understood why people can have thought that the sensible N. was near to madness.

People complained, too, about the end of that novel, when she is raped by a stranger in the garage, and finds herself somehow in harmony with this event, or relieved by it. What I had in mind was ending with her in the state of mind when everything bad that can happen has happened, leaving her free of further dread. But alas, some people took me to be saying that women like to be raped. I think now I would have to choose some other, less politically significant act of violence to make the point.

I had in mind that the rapist was the Famous Inspector, but the editor at Knopf convinced me that that was "too much," so I left the matter unresolved. I believe I have a tendency to go too far with endings, and someone always talks me out of the last little sting in the tail I had planned. In *Persian Nights,* when the heroine, Chloe Fowler, finally gets on a plane to go home, I had a sentence which would make you realize she had got on the wrong plane (there being great chaos in the Tehran airport) and was going to end up in Geneva. Of course this wouldn't have changed anything—she would have just gotten back to the United States a little later, with some inconvenience—it wasn't really important at all. So I acceded to editorial inquietude and took it out.

I think I have been too docile about titles. I forget what I planned to call *Fair Game,* but it wasn't that. My next novel, *Loving Hands at Home,* I had planned to call *Being Alma,* after a character that has a kind of inspirational significance to the heroine, Karen. Alma was the bad girl in her hometown, the one who found out about sex and economic realities before anybody else. *Loving Hands* was an early version of a novel that many women writers have written since— the bored or disappointed housewife novel. A particular favorite of mine in this genre is Sheila Ballantine's *Norma Jean the Termite Queen*—not a title that does justice to this wonderfully witty and trenchant novel. Another title of my own that I was made to change was *Aspiradora.* This became *Lying Low,* which I think is a pretty good title too, but I will always think of the novel as *Aspiradora.* This word, with its reverberations of "aspirations" and its specific meaning, vacuum cleaner, refers to one of the central characters, the Brazilian Ouida, who is the cleaning lady and admirer of American manners.

It was with this novel, *Lying Low,* that I finally stopped feeling the ghost of Henry James glaring over my shoulder in disapproval at the mélange of points of view I find myself using, and became comfortable suiting myself in this matter. I know what James said, of course, and deeply revere his strictures on most things. I almost love his prefaces better than his novels. Almost no other writer has left so many directions and interesting observations about the art of novel-writing. I also love Ford Madox Ford's manifesto, in his biography of Conrad. I came under the spell of Ford's *The Good Soldier* when I was writing *The Shadow Knows.* This elusive novel of passion and menace is so artfully constructed that I took a week and outlined it, according to a complicated system of notation I devised, not merely noting what happened but isolating the themes, the points of climax, the chronology, and so on. This was so helpful to me in understanding structure that I then outlined *The Shadow,* and later, *Lying Low.* In between writing these two books, I worked with Stanley Kubrick, the director, on the screenplay of his film *The Shining.* Here, too, we worked very hard on the outline before ever writing any of the scenes, and this left me convinced that outlines (not hard, inflexible, calculating ones) are indispensable, if one has the patience to do them, as a means of perfecting the structure, and of understanding a lot about a novel before plunging in and making mistakes by rushing ahead, the way one does with one's first novel, innocent of all the formal decisions that will have to be made.

I became wary of speaking of the outline, for instance to a workshop of creative-writing students, because it seems to be in many minds a kind of commercial gimmick, something you are told to do in "how-to" books, or by agents or publishers who tell you to submit three chapters and an outline. No one would understand my outlines—they don't tell any of the events or even, often, the subject, and they look like this:

CcDccQ R s'1

In a new novel, one I've just finished, called *Health and Happiness* (as yet no one has suggested I change the title), I got interested in the problem of, or task of, trying to write a true comedy of manners. Thus the issues became tone and pace (in addition, of course, to characters, point of view, and what actually happens). The subject is indicated in the title, the connection between health and happiness, worked out in a hospital setting. This setting, I found, was fraught with pitfalls, mainly the difficulty of avoiding melodrama, for hospitals are implicitly melodramatic, full of death, pain, and crisis. When a novel isn't yet published (at which time I can forget about it), I am still in the disappointed frame of mind in which the writer, faced with what she has wrought, can't help but compare it to what she had in mind. Inevitably the novel you end up with is different than the ideal composition you were planning—I wanted mine to be sprightly, very sharp about doctors and their foibles and the medical profession in general, and women—their wives, nurses, and so on. Susan Cheever has a novel whose title I greatly wanted for my own: *Doctors and Women.* I am sure our two novels are nothing alike, but I haven't dared to read hers, in case of some similarity which would have made me start mine over!

I became aware in writing *Health and Happiness* that I was touching on matters I explored in the early novel I haven't yet mentioned, *Burning,* which I also thought of as being a novel of manners, and of place, Los Angeles. It takes place in one day, the day of a fire, one of those richly metaphorical fires they are always having in Los Angeles which consume the houses of rich people and so on. I've always been fond of this novel—more than other people were, I have to admit. It did teach me, though, that it is unwise to write about Los Angeles, or to set things there, if you want people in other parts of the country to believe that the events and conditions you are describing have any general relevance. Having lived there, I myself have a great affection for Los Angeles novels—Alison Lurie's wonderful *Nowhere City,* and all the novels of Carolyn See, for example.

Besides novels, I've written various essays and two biographies. People often ask which I prefer, and whether I find it hard to write both nonfiction and fiction. The answer to the latter is no. I enjoy writing essays, I suppose because I am an opinionated person and it is a great luxury to be enabled to express these opinions and preach a little in a form more concise than the concealed didacticism that is (always, anybody's) novel.

Biographies are another matter. I liked writing *Lesser Lives,* the story of a circle of minor Victorian figures, at the center of which was a woman, Mary Ellen Meredith, the daughter of Thomas Love Peacock, wife of George Meredith, and lover of Henry Wallis, a minor pre-Raphaelite. The premise was that minor figures have lives which seem important to them if not to history. The fun of writing this book was that I had only the tiniest traces of research, little packets of letters that no one had ever read before, some wills, and a tattered pink parasol. It was a work of imaginative sympathy, I suppose. In the case of Dashiell Hammett, my other biographical subject, I experienced a problem common with biographers, a failure of imaginative sympathy. I would find myself becoming censorious over his alcoholism, the waste of his talent, his tendencies to beat up women and skip out on his hotel bills, and would have to talk myself into remembering the gallant things about his response to his sad life. With Hammett, I let him speak for himself (by quoting abundantly from his letters) and made very few attempts at interpretation myself.

Because certain questions are always asked after a reading—How, with what, do you write? How do you think up your subjects?—I assume these are interesting questions. I know that writers are interested in such matters, and among ourselves will discuss word processors and such. I remember getting a letter years ago, before such machines, from Alison Lurie, which said "a typewriter ribbon can be revived, in an emergency, by soaking it in vegetable oil. Pass it on." Now I write in longhand or on a little electronic typewriter, a portable light gadget. I have three of them—one at my home in San Francisco, one in a little writing room I rent, and one in Paris where I have an apartment. I write on yellow paper—I don't know why that seems important. I have a friend who writes on pink or blue paper—I never could do that. Blue! A color I particularly detest.

Some writers start from a character or even a title, or something glimpsed by accident, as Henry James describes doing. But I start from an idea, a sort of thematic notion. I might think of it as A Novel about Americans Abroad in the Third World—this became *Persian Nights.* I have mentioned how I thought of *The Shadow Knows. Lying Low* was to be about the issues of involvement and commitment. *Health and Happiness,* as I have said, about modern medicine. All these are political themes, and in my own mind I am kind of a political novelist. I am always surprised when critics find a tone of tragedy or romance, though it is fair to say that I try for all these things at once, for I believe that a novel can be funny and serious at once, and should be. All the writers I admire are funny and serious—Waugh and Kafka, Austen and Dickens, to speak of the classics. The greatest writers have all been funny. I suppose a writer doesn't have to choose a category, but you do find yourself put into one by others after the fact, and I guess mine is a sort of serio-comic satiric category. That is fine with me, but I hope it doesn't mean that my work isn't taken seriously, for it is seriously meant.

My impression is that, though different writers find the genesis of a novel in different ways, all are alike in their sense of having the work inside them in some potential form. The analogy to gestation is very exact. The work must be born to be known. One's sense of it beforehand is strong, yet so subvocal, so unconscious, and often so different from what the reader will find it to be about that the possibilities of misunderstanding, between the writer and the work, and between the writer and the reader, are very great indeed.

Because the process of writing *Health and Happiness* is fresh in my mind, I can recapitulate something of my thinking at the beginning. I knew I wanted to write about doctors. What about them? Well, the relationship of doctors and nurses, doctors and patients—doctors and women. The erotic power and the power of fear that they have over others. The complexities of their job (I am married to a doctor). Something of the situation of modern medicine, its moral situation.

Once you think of all the things a novel is to be about, you still have to embody it in a story. Between these two steps, a great painful chasm, a gap, a silence can prevail, at least for me. As in darkness, I grope toward the story, something to hang the aboutness on. I think the process is opposite for some writers—they think of a gripping story first, and then the complexities and moral ramifications develop as they write.

In *Health and Happiness* I hit upon using an experience of my own, one day when I woke up and noticed that one of my arms was swollen up. From here it was easy to find a heroine to whom this is to happen. But, if she is the patient, she won't be able to see and know a lot of things around the hospital—someone else will be needed. For this, I found Mimi Franklin, the coordinator of volunteer services. And what is a doctor novel without a doctor hero? Here I invent Philip Watts, the head doctor. In this way, little by little, the characters assemble on the stage. I change their names a dozen times. Eventually they tell me which is their real name. Almost all novelists testify to the curious experience of having characters refuse to do what you want them to, and change the course of a novel. This has often happened to me. Mimi, the volunteer coordinator, remained mysterious to me until a friend pointed out that she was exceptionally tall, and that accounted for her shyness and reserve. That helped me to realize other things about her. In this novel, Philip, the main male character, seemed to see things most closely to the way I would see them, though normally I feel this affinity more for the female characters. Of course the writer is really all the characters, not just the Emma Bovary character.

People sometimes ask about, or assume, feminism in my works. I in turn assume that any nice woman is a feminist in some sense. I don't set out to explicate feminist themes in my work though, and I object to things that concern half the human race (all the human race really) being relegated to the status of political issue instead of being seen as an aspect of human experience, of concern and interest to everybody. If you are a woman writer, you will naturally see things from a female perspective, your experience having been shaped in that way, and that inclines you to views which other people often think are "political" when they are merely literal.

I have always found this odd. For instance, because women tend to have a satirical view of men, and you are writing a scene in which women talk about men, and you put down what real women would say, people imagine it is you satirizing men. To be fair, I believe that the same thing happens to male authors—a notable example being Leonard Michaels's *The Men's Club,* in which the author, meaning to expose the crudity and poverty of some men's emotional lives, was accused of himself holding the sexist views his characters held.

I suppose that the moral views and emotional state of the author are always a kind of subtext in reading a novel. Because the writer is hiding behind a construction, the reader feels impelled to try to spy her out, a situation different from what happens in poetry, or in the essay, where the writer tries to explain her views as clearly as she can—but to begin to discourse on the general, instead of the particulars of my work, is, I think, a sign to myself that I have said as much as I can.

NINE BEGINNINGS

MARGARET ATWOOD

1. *Why do you write?*

I've begun this piece nine times. I've junked each beginning.

I hate writing about my writing. I almost never do it. Why am I doing it now? Because I said I would. I got a letter. I wrote back *no*. Then I was at a party and the same person was there. It's harder to refuse in person. Saying *yes* had something to do with being nice, as women are taught to be, and something to do with being helpful, which we are also taught. Being helpful to women, giving a pint of blood. With not claiming the sacred prerogatives, the touch-me-not self-protectiveness of the artist, with not being selfish. With conciliation, with doing your bit, with appeasement. I was well brought up. I have trouble ignoring social obligations. Saying you'll write about your writing is a social obligation. It's not an obligation to the writing.

2. *Why do you write?*

I've junked each of nine beginnings. They seemed beside the point. Too assertive, too pedagogical, too frivolous or belligerent, too falsely wise. As if I had some special self-revelation that would encourage others, or some special knowledge to impart, some pithy saying that would act like a talisman for the driven, the obsessed. But I have no such talismans. If I did, I would not continue, myself, to be so driven and obsessed.

3. *Why do you write?*

I hate writing about my writing because I have nothing to say about it. I have nothing to say about it because I can't remember what goes on when I'm doing it. That time is like small pieces cut out of my brain. It's not time I myself have lived. I can remember the details of the rooms and places where I've written, the circumstances, the other things I did before and after, but not the process itself. Writing about writing requires self-consciousness; writing itself requires the abdication of it.

4. *Why do you write?*

There are a lot of things that can be said about what goes on around the edges of writing. Certain ideas you may have, certain motivations, grand designs that don't get carried out. I can talk about bad reviews, about sexist reactions to my writing, about making an idiot of myself on television shows. I can talk about books that failed, that never got finished, and about why they failed. The one that had too many characters, the one that had too many layers of time, red herrings that diverted me when what I really wanted to get at was something else, a certain corner of the visual world, a certain voice, an inarticulate landscape.

I can talk about the difficulties that women encounter as writers. For instance, if you're a woman writer, sometime, somewhere, you will be asked: *Do you think of yourself as a writer first, or as a woman first?* Look out. Whoever asks this hates and fears both writing and women.

Many of us, in my generation at least, ran into teachers or male writers or other defensive jerks who told us women could not really write because they couldn't be truck drivers or Marines and therefore didn't understand the seamier side of life, which included sex with women. We were told we wrote like housewives, or else we were treated like honorary men, as if to be a good writer was to suppress the female.

Such pronouncements used to be made as if they were the simple truth. Now they're questioned. Some things have changed for the better, but not all. There's a lack of self-confidence that gets instilled very early in many young girls, before writing is even seen as a possibility. You need a certain amount of nerve to be a writer, an almost physical nerve, the kind you need to walk a log across a river. The horse throws you and you get back on the horse. I learned to swim by being dropped into the water. You need to know you can sink, and survive it. Girls should be allowed to play in the mud. They should be released from the obligations of perfection. Some of your writing, at least, should be as evanescent as play.

A ratio of failures is built into the process of writing. The wastebasket has evolved for a reason. Think of it as the altar of the Muse Oblivion, to whom you sacrifice your botched first drafts, the tokens of your human imperfection. She is the tenth Muse, the one without whom none of the others can function. The gift she offers you is the freedom of the second chance. Or as many chances as you'll take.

5. *Why do you write?*

In the mid-eighties I began a sporadic journal. Today I went back through it, looking for something I could dig out and fob off as pertinent, instead of writing this piece about writing. But it was useless. There was nothing in it about the actual composition of anything I've written over the past six years. Instead there are exhortations to myself—to get up earlier, to walk more, to resist lures and distractions. *Drink more water,* I find. *Go to bed earlier.* There were lists of how many pages I'd written per day, how many I'd retyped, how many yet to go. Other than that, there was nothing but descriptions of rooms, accounts of what we'd cooked and/or eaten and with whom, letters written and received, notable sayings of children, birds and animals seen, the weather. What came up in the garden. Illnesses, my own and those of others. Deaths, births. Nothing about writing.

January 1, 1984. Blakeny, England. As of today, I have about 130 pp. of the novel done and it's just beginning to take shape & reach the point at which I feel that it exists and can be finished and may be worth it. I work in the bedroom of the big house, and here, in the sitting room, with the wood fire in the fireplace and the coke fire in the dilapidated Roeburn in the kitchen. As usual I'm too cold, which is better than being too hot—today is grey, warm for the time of year, damp. If I got up earlier maybe I would work more, but I might just spend more time procrastinating—as now.

And so on.

6. *Why do you write?*

You learn to write by reading and writing, writing and reading. As a craft it's acquired through the apprentice system, but you choose your own teachers. Sometimes they're alive, sometimes dead.

As a vocation, it involves the laying on of hands. You receive your vocation and in your turn you must pass it on. Perhaps you will do this only through your work, perhaps in other ways. Either way, you're part of a community, the community of writers, the community of storytellers that stretches back through time to the beginning of human society.

As for the particular human society to which you yourself belong—sometimes you'll feel you're speaking for it, sometimes—when it's taken an unjust form—against it, or for that other community, the community of the oppressed, the exploited, the voiceless. Either way, the pressures on you will be intense; in other countries, perhaps fatal. But even here—speak "for women," or for any other group which is feeling the boot, and there will be many at hand, both for and against, to tell you to shut up, or to say what they want you to say, or to say it a different way. Or to save them. The billboard awaits you, but if you succumb to its temptations you'll end up two-dimensional.

Tell what is yours to tell. Let others tell what is theirs.

7. *Why do you write?*

Why are we so addicted to causality? *Why do* you *write?* (Treatise by child psychologist, mapping your formative traumas. Conversely: palm-reading, astrology and genetic studies, pointing to the stars, fate, heredity.) *Why do you write?* (That is, why not do something useful instead?) If you were a doctor, you could tell some acceptable moral tale about how you put Band-Aids on your cats as a child, how you've always longed to cure suffering. No one can argue with that. But writing? What is it *for?*

Some possible answers: *Why does the sun shine? In the face of the absurdity of modern society, why do anything else? Because I'm a writer. Because I want to discover the patterns in the chaos of time. Because I must. Because someone has to bear witness. Why do you read?* (This last is tricky: maybe they don't.) *Because I wish to forge in the smithy of my soul the uncreated conscience of my race. Because I wish to make an axe to break the frozen sea within.* (These have been used, but they're good.)

If at a loss, perfect the shrug. Or say: *It's better than working in a bank.* Or say: *For fun.* If you say this, you won't be believed, or else you'll be dismissed as trivial. Either way, you'll have avoided the question.

8. *Why do you write?*

Not long ago, in the course of clearing some of the excess paper out of my workroom, I opened a filing cabinet drawer I hadn't looked into for years. In it was a bundle of loose sheets, folded, creased, and grubby, tied up with leftover string. It consisted of things I'd written in the late fifties, in high school and the early years of university. There were scrawled, inky poems, about snow, despair, and the Hungarian Revolution. There were short stories dealing with girls who'd had to get married, and dispirited, mousy-haired high-school English teachers—to end up as either was at that time my vision of Hell—typed finger-by-finger on an ancient machine that made all the letters half-red.

There I am, then, back in grade twelve, going through the writers' magazines after I'd finished my French Composition homework, typing out my lugubrious poems and my grit-filled stories. (I was big on grit. I had an eye for lawn-litter and dog turds on sidewalks. In these stories it was usually snowing damply, or raining; at the very least there was slush. If it was summer, the heat and humidity were always wiltingly high and my characters had sweat marks under their arms; if it was spring, wet clay stuck to their feet. Though some would say all this was just normal Toronto weather.)

In the top right-hand corners of some of these, my hopeful seventeen-year-old self had typed, "First North American Rights Only." I was not sure what "First North American Rights" were; I put it in because the writing magazines said you should. I was at that time an aficionado of writing magazines, having no one else to turn to for professional advice.

If I were an archeologist, digging through the layers of old paper that mark the eras in my life as a writer, I'd have found, at the lowest or Stone Age level—say around ages five to seven—a few poems and stories, unremarkable precursors of all my frenetic later scribbling. (Many children write at that age, just as many children draw. The strange thing is that so few of them go on to become writers or painters.) After that there's a great blank. For eight years, I simply didn't write. Then, suddenly, and with no missing links in between, there's a wad of manuscripts. One week I wasn't a writer, the next I was.

Who did I think I was, to be able to get away with this? What did I think I was doing? How did I get that way? To these questions I still have no answers.

9. *Why do you write?*

There's the blank page, and the thing that obsesses you. There's the story that wants to take you over and there's your resistance to it. There's your longing to get out of this, this servitude, to play hooky, to do anything else: wash the laundry, see a movie. There are words and their inertias, their biases, their insufficiencies, their glories. There are the risks you take and your loss of nerve, and the help that comes when you're least expecting it. There's the laborious revision, the scrawled-over, crumpled-up pages that drift across the floor like spilled litter. There's the one sentence you know you will save.

Next day there's the blank page. You give yourself up to it like a sleepwalker. Something goes on that you can't remember afterwards. You look at what you've done. It's hopeless.

You begin again. It never gets any easier.

THE HOUSE THAT JILL BUILT

RITA DOVE

Tamarra hunts me down to invite me to lunch. "I'd like to compare our creative processes," she begins. No preamble. Tamarra is a photographer teaching in the School of Art. She also reads voraciously and has required Annie Dillard's *Living by Fiction* in her graduate seminar because she believes art students can learn something about their creative activity by studying other genres. She suggests that we bring our graduate workshops together and see what happens.

Despite my crammed schedule, I agree to an extra evening meeting. This woman's cut-the-crap-let's-get-down-to-the-bones approach appeals to me; it reminds me, here in Arizona, of the East Coast and the edge there that makes intellectual inquiry so urgent. We discuss creativity over soybean burgers and power milkshakes. I had never realized how much serendipity is involved with photography, how the perfect image may please the eye but somehow disappears when it enters the lens; or how the portrait photographer learns to be journalist and counselor, coaxing subjects to reveal their secrets, keeping them at ease while the tripod is set up and rolls of film are changed. All that business in the darkroom seems so much like my process of revision; I wish I could turn on a red light when I'm at work in my study.

I'm sure our classes are getting something from the exchange, but it's patently clear to me that this extra meeting is also a way for us to become better acquainted by watching each other work. The deal is: if we respect each other professionally, perhaps we'll take a stab at becoming friends.

This is my first relationship with a woman that is based on the rules commonly associated with men. Brought together by our jobs, we pool resources, then ideas; later we drag our husbands to each other's houses for dinner, and while the men sit about discussing Reaganomics and pool chemicals, Tamarra and I chew over everything from Jungian symbols in religion to the morality of an artist toward her subject to violent mother-child dreams.

It's a new semester. Tamarra has horned into an impossible agenda, this time with an irresistible long-term project. We agree to meet weekly to explore the connections between image and word. The "Photo Collaborative Facility" at the university is interested in producing a letterpress book of my poems with Tamarra's images, transferred to print by collotype, a nineteenth-century photographic process.

I'm in the middle of a dry period—not a writer's block, just a dearth of creative activity. I've just sent back the first set of proofs for my next book of poems and am awaiting the second set; no wonder I can't write. Maybe this project will give me a push in a new direction . . .

We're determined to make this collaboration unusual, not another look-at-the-pretty-pictures-ignore-the-text-and-put-on-the-coffee-table book. We want to collaborate from the bottom up; we want to make a book grounded on the idea of working together, woman and woman. But how to begin? "We'll just see what happens," Tamarra replies, scribbling a date for next week in her red organizer.

Before Tamarra arrives I am frantically leafing through old note-books, looking for a clue to—what? I don't know, anything, a thread that links the disparity in the poems of several books, some motif that will leap from the page like a red line of reasoning and make all this eternal fumbling clear. I re-read my books—a depressing exercise I recommend to nobody. Why are so many women in my poems standing in rooms or at the threshold to rooms? Why are they so wistful? Why aren't they *doing* anything? Do I live only in my mind? And in the poem "Upon Reading Hölderlin on the Patio with the Aid of a Dictionary" . . . why, at the moment of revelation, do I "step out of my body"? Am I afraid my body will hold me down? And yet I don't feel stapled to the earth; that is, I don't consider gravity consciously, I don't think of it as a grounding.

Tamarra brings two cameras and a plastic bag stuffed with film because, step one, I have agreed to serve as the model in order to better understand a photographer's "field work," as well as experience what it is like to study oneself as a visual object. We are both too tired to look for a common subject; we don't want to go anywhere. We sit down with glasses of iced tea on the patio. "Why not *here?*" Tamarra suggests. I look at our ragtag yard. The scrap-lumber fence, nailed up by the previous owner, is a soft weathered gray; I like the gaps and knotholes but my husband periodically swears and closes them up, furiously nailing more scrap lumber over the slits. The fence is a patchwork of human enterprise.

"Why not?" I nod. As a city girl who can sprint twenty gates through O'Hare but who'd collapse at the mere mention of hiking South Mountain, this suits me just fine. The backyard is as much nature as I can stand. In fact, last summer I spent the first week back from Europe waking up at 5 A.M., wired up with no place to go; so I'd take a chaise longue out to the side yard to "commune with nature," but, between the bees and the distant drone of the cheese factory five blocks away, I never lasted more than thirty minutes.

We troop into the side yard and Tamarra shoots a roll of warm-up poses which I call "Ruminating Author Gazes Off into the Distance." The yard's a mess, with Aviva's sun-bleached tricycle shoved against a tree and a burst water hose snaking through overgrown weeds. Tamarra exclaims over textures and the interplay of light and shadow, but I'm acutely self-conscious—what if these shots actually appear somewhere? Then I hear a rustle of paper, a squeal coming around the corner of the house, and I stiffen instinctively, not daring to look at Aviva rushing into the photo session with her crayon masterpieces.

"That was terrific!" Tamarra says later. We've switched to beer. "Just as Aviva came around the corner your body got tense, but your eyes were still trying to hold the horizon. And that tricycle and the holes in the fence . . . perfect!"

I was afraid she'd say something like that.

Tamarra brings the contact sheets. God, the lawn mower was showing! I'm mortified. But even on the contact print I can see that the composition is interesting, the stiffness in my pose weirdly appropriate to the shabby domesticity.

She's also brought along several quilts. I don't own a quilt; my grandmother was the last member of our family to make them and the last quilt, faded and worn through, is in my mother's cedar closet. I can't wait to lie on these and suggest spreading them under the serrated shadows of the dwarf palm tree.

"I've got an idea you won't like," Tamarra says, spreading the quilt between the palm and plate-glass window. "I'd like to photograph you both—you and Aviva—nude. You know, a kind of a variation on the Madonna and Child stuff."

Oh, dear, here we go. I think of Vanessa Williams and the Mormons in the neighboring town who watch the university for "signs of immorality." I remember my father forbidding us to read *National Geographic*—not because there were photographs of naked women, but because the only naked women were dark-skinned; evidently Third World nudity did not offend Western sensibilities.

"All right—but only if nothing shows."

Nude in the backyard in the middle of the day! What a luxury! The only time I'd been nude outdoors (not counting beaches in Yugoslavia and northern Germany, where it's common) was one summer night when I sprang out of bed to hang up the laundry I'd forgotten. It was delicious, standing under the palo verde tree with nothing between my skin and the stars but the desert air. I dallied until footsteps from the alley sent me scurrying back inside.

Tamarra offers Aviva a quarter if she'll stay still, and like an exemplary capitalist she curls into the most provocative infant positions. Where'd she learn to do that? I find myself relaxing in spite of Tamarra's chatter (which is meant to relax me). When was the last time I spent hours doing nothing? During breastfeeding maybe, when there was a legitimate excuse for lying down to float for a while . . .

That night I study the contact sheets. The lawn mower *did* look kinda good where it stood. In fact, if I considered the scene objectively, the disorder of the yard had a beauty of its own. A beautiful lawn mower? What an outrageous idea! But why not? In a notebook I scribble:

> From the beautiful lawn mower
> float curls of evaporated gasoline;
> the hinged ax of the butterfly pauses.

On second thought, I transfer the lines to a clean sheet of notebook paper, about five lines down: they belong to the middle of a poem; somehow I know this. Then I slip the piece of paper into a green plastic folder and put the folder back in the drawer.

For years I thought the only "proper" way to write was to start a poem and plug away at it until it was done—sort of like finishing all the food on your plate at dinner. I worried my poems like a dog does a bone. Then, one afternoon about seven years ago, I was wandering through a stationery store in West Berlin. (Like many writers on the eternal search for the Perfect Writing Implement, I haunt stationery stores.) I discovered an array of plastic folders, closed on two sides, that came in clear red and purple and yellow and blue. I bought the entire rainbow. And suddenly everything changed. If a poem I was working on eluded completion, I'd slip the pages into one of the colored folders. Instead of producing whole poems I began to collect fragments and let them grow in the dark. This way I could work on several poems at once; some, of course, were doomed to remain fragments, and some would complete themselves within a month or ten weeks or two years. Now when I sit down to write, I first spread out the folders, choose the color that suits my "mood," and leaf through it until something strikes me. I'll work on that fragment until I get stuck, and then I'll go on to another poem in that folder, or switch colors. After weeks of fiddling I often complete two or three poems on the same day.

I like to compare this process to the housewife who can prepare a four-course dinner on two burners while changing the baby's diaper, smearing a peanut-butter sandwich for her five-year-old, and setting the table. Or it is like the hostess who balances the shyness of one guest with the drunkenness of another while passing the canapés. After all, the skill of juggling has been required of women for centuries; women were raised to please others, to put their demands on the back burner instead of wrestling their desires to the ground.

After a longer hesitation, I pull out the red folder (the one I secretly call *The Hot Line*) and leaf through the contents: angry poems, war poems, fragments petering off in despair or choking on bile. But nothing already written in this folder touches the niggling patch of anxiety that has been with me since . . . well, since the afternoon. Something about the way Aviva had stretched out, comfortable in her nakedness, while I hunched over her, fighting the memory of my first *National Geographic:* the shame I felt at witnessing this full-color delectation of "the exotic," the rage as I understood how erotic fascination could replace any liberal call for empathy and acceptance of the other.

Altogether too hot to handle. I put the folder back in the drawer, but even then I knew I would have to bring it out again—although it would take half a year before the photograph was made that spawned "Genetic Expedition," a poem Tamarra praises for getting down to the "nitty-gritty."

REGISTER!!!

****

GYNOCRITICS: WOMAN AS WRITER.
(ENG 547, Section B)

Studies in contemporary poetry written by women, with emphasis on the psychodynamics of female creativity.

Tuesday 1:40–4:30
Professor Rita Dove

****

* Is there such a thing as a "female language"?
* Can there be a "male muse"?
* Why are women often described by men as an aspect of nature ("virgin territory," "my little chickadee," "you cow") and why do men set themselves apart from nature?
* Are there themes and metaphors common to feminine experience?
* What can influence syntax and perception? Have the traditional "occupations" of women, which often interrupt concentration, led to different ways of organizing thought?

Thirty female graduate students! And no one complains about the workload; in fact, they want extra meetings, extra reading lists, more of everything. So far the following questions have cropped up:

1. Does the strategy of Prufrock work for an aging female? Is there a male counterpart to the mermaids that isn't ludicrous?

2. Is the moon always a sister, or is it an opponent? What sex are the stars? How do they compare to the moon?

3. Flowers: Are they potent symbolically, or have they been romanticized out of existence?

4. Why are we so afraid of smells?

5. Men often dissect a woman in order to "praise" her. ("My mistress' eyes are nothing like the sun . . .") Do women do this to men? Do women do this to themselves? Do men do this to themselves?

6. What do you fear the most in the world? What did women fear most in the past?

7. What about orgasm? Does the fact that a woman has to let go and open up—whereas the man bears down, takes control, holds back—does this count for anything in the general experience of emotion?

And we're only in the fourth week of the semester!

The lesson plan says Week 6: *The Labours of Beauty.* The assignment: Come as you would never want to be seen in public. I start class fifteen minutes late so that they have time to change; the giggles and shrieks from the adjacent bathroom remind me of high school basketball games. Then they troop in, and the confessions begin: one married student, still fighting for thighs like a fourteen-year-old, wears her bathing suit. An older student is radiant in the rainbow caftan she wears only at home because "fat people aren't supposed to wear bright colors." Yet another is dressed like a hippie, scarves and beads and buffalo sandals, because that's the time she felt really alive.

My disguise is simple: to do nothing. No makeup, hair pulled back in a braid, the dullest, slackest dress I could find, glasses instead of contacts—the dowdy schoolmarm. By the end of the session, I feel so good that I forget and go into the English office to get my mail. The secretaries are aghast, call others in to look. By the time I bike home for dinner I am self-conscious again. Chantal, our friend visiting from Paris, looks up from her book, shocked. "You went to the university like that?"

Her utter disdain plunges me into doubt. What was I trying to prove, anyway? Had I gone too far in my zeal to be innovative? It had felt good to bare my obsession in class; in fact, we'd all felt good, honest at last—but what about our reentry into the world? How did it feel to take off the rainbow caftan again and hide it in a satchel until you got back to the safety of your own bedroom? How would the student in the bathing suit react if she ran into another member of the class at the mall, clad in her sensible skirt? Perhaps I had done these students a disservice by cracking them open—for now they had placed their trust in me, and how could I protect them? How, after peeling away the protective layers, could we put them back?

All winter Tamarra and I work like maniacs. I finish the poem with the lawn mower and call it "The Other Side of the House," Tamarra pulls two achingly beautiful prints from the Madonna on the Quilt series. For those photos I write "Pastoral," a poem on breastfeeding. Tamarra comes by when I'm not home so that she can convince Aviva to be photographed in a swimsuit holding a dead grasshopper in her palm. She makes another appointment to photograph the yard "naked," without people—the empty hammock, the broken rocking horse. I see the contact sheets and write a poem about dolls instead, which sends Tamarra out to the yard to fling several of Aviva's dolls in various positions of abandon on the (still unmown) grass. I write the rocking horse poem. And so on, into the spring, squeezed between workshops and job-search committees.

All spring semester the graduates of the Gynocritics class stop by for critiques of new poems. Many of them are floundering, hurt by the lack of response their work receives in other workshops. In general their new poems are not as polished as their former work, thus susceptible to the standard artillery of peer critique—economy of words, objectivity, specificity of image—and yet on the whole these new poems are more interesting, more connected. How to tell them this without making them combative? "My body needs air," one student writes, and it is so perfect, this line, that it alone is worth a semester's agony.

West Berlin, September

My dear Tamarra,

Is there life after a Pulitzer? Well, yes, there is—a glittery, breath-taking-in-flashes life; but the inner state is fraught with dread, anxiety, and a terrifying emptiness. Even lassitude. (Because you're an Easterner, I know when I complain like this that you won't take it as an international emergency.) I suppose I was asked the question "Are you afraid that getting the Pulitzer (at such a young age!) will affect the way you write from now on?" a few too many times. It is damn hard to face the blank page (or even one that's been scribbled on), especially when people expect you to. If it hadn't been for your insistence, dear lady, the Aviva series would have never been completed, I would have written no poems worth publishing since that bloody prize, and then where would I be now? I thank you. And I miss you.

But sabbaticals were made in heaven. Now we're in Berlin for three weeks. We've installed Aviva in a wonderfully chaotic *Kinderladen*. (At first she thought we were going to trade her in at the

"Kid's Store"; we explained that "Kinderladen" stood for day-care center.) We drop her off at ten every morning, then walk to a friend's architect's office, where we work in two unoccupied rooms overlooking Kurfürstendamm. With free time until 3 P.M. and nothing to distract us, we're forced to write. (Why is what one longs to do such a torture when one "has to" do it?) After writing like crazy for the first three days, I hit a snag and all the self-doubts crept back—no, swooped in—and I spent a sour afternoon storming up and down Kurfürstendamm, blazing into boutiques and trying on clothes I had no intention of buying. Then that evening, Fred in his infinite wisdom began joking about Rilke and the Sonnets to Orpheus, suggesting that I write Sonnets to Diana. "Not to Diana, but to Demeter," I replied, and this morning I dashed down the beginnings to five sonnets (would you have believed that I'd ever write *sonnets*!?), and they're about missing periods and trying to lose weight and all that nitty-gritty stuff. So it goes—

Diary entry:

> *What happens when a writer doesn't want to write anymore? When the progression of fingers across the keyboard is like an old dry horse hitched to the millstone, blinders and yoke lashed, the only path between day and nightfall one's own scoured rut of circling footsteps? This is of no use to anyone, if anything is of use, if utility is to be more than what one suspects it is—the plank across the mudhole.*

The sonnets are stalled. I've become self-conscious; after all, how far can a Greek goddess lead a Black poet? It's an old stumbling block: I'll be lost in the luxurious foliage of Western civilization when a passage from *Lady Chatterley's Lover* will bring me up short—"never a woman who'd really 'come' naturally with a man: except black women, and somehow, well, we're white men: and they're a bit like mud"—with the brutal reminder that the culture I was feeding on had no interest in nourishing me.

The only useful method I've found to combat this is to insist upon inclusion; in other words, to rewrite the tradition. If, as a woman, I can connect with the Demeter-Kore myth but still feel something is missing, it's my task to find the missing link or, failing that, to invent it. I scour the bookstores in West Berlin until I find her, the other Demeter. Her name is Isis, Queen of Egypt.

Back home in Arizona—the telephone ringing, ringing, everybody wants a reading and I feel like a fraud. Why? Because I haven't written enough, not six months' worth at any rate. (And what is six months' worth of poetry?) Besides, I still have half of a sabbatical left and this is the half the writing is supposed to "happen" in.

But there's our daughter's fifth birthday to plan. She wants a Siamese cat on the one hand and a "princess dress" on the other. I recognize the influence of Disney videos (in this case, *The Lady and the Tramp* and *Cinderella*) but say nothing. Instead, I spend an afternoon in the fabric shop, choosing the sturdiest pink lace for the skirt and white pique for the bodice; then I stop by the public library for a book on how to sew lace.

"You're out of your mind," my husband says late that evening, watching me on hands and knees, scissoring along the pattern pieces spread over the living-room floor. "What are you wasting your time for? You should be writing."

"This is fun," I answer, checking the carpet for stray straight pins. "Besides, I always make her a new dress for her birthday."

"But lace? Come on, Rita; she's turning five. Thirty minutes in that concoction and it'll be in shreds."

"So what? At least she's had the dress she wanted. And she won't have to stand around like a porcelain doll, afraid to sit down because the organdy petticoat will prick her legs." I make a mental note to cover all the exposed seams with bias tape.

He shrugs, turns back to *PC Magazine.* "Do what you want; it's your sabbatical."

"Unfair," I call out. "You have your video equipment, I have sewing." I want to remind him of the long poem I've been working on with sewing as the central metaphor and cite this dress as field work, but decide it might be a tactical error to bring up writing again.

On the night before the birthday the dress is finished. As Aviva tries it on, we approach the pet question. Pets and travel don't mix; doesn't she like visiting Oma in Germany every summer? (Oh, but haven't I held a lifelong grudge against parents who refused to harbor even a single grasshopper after the guinea pig my brother and I caught in the garage died a terrible and obvious death of dehydration? Don't my brother and I argue to this day over whose turn it was to feed him?) After careful consideration, our daughter gives up the idea of a dog or cat and agrees to a turtle and some goldfish. Secretly, we decide on the turtle, with goldfish to come if she proves responsible. Off to the pet store we go the next morning, two intellectuals who don't know that you can't buy turtles in January, even in Arizona. "They're hibernating," the pet shop owner explains, smiling gently at our ignorance. "Come back in March."

So it'll be goldfish. I've never liked goldfish because they turn belly-up-black when they die and are flushed down the toilet. An actress doing a guest appearance at the Freie Volksbuehne in West Berlin once told me how her goldfish froze in his bowl when she had left the windows open in the middle of winter; then her boyfriend came over and slowly warmed the bowl over the electric burner until the fish swam again. I jotted down the episode in one of my notebooks and was surprised when it emerged two years later in a poem called "Dusting," in which a housewife reminiscing about her courting years remembers coming "home / from a dance, the front door / blown open and the parlor / in snow," and that instinctively "she rushed / the bowl to the stove, watched / as the locket of ice / dissolved and he / swam free." That poem slipped out like the fish, freeing an entire book of poems.

The first time I remember writing in the headlong fashion bespeaking "inspiration," that pure electric streak, was in third or fourth grade. In school we had spelling lessons—those horrible lists of words to memorize week after week, and the boring exercises geared to teach us how to use each word correctly. I would finish the exercises as quickly as possible; then I'd look around for something to occupy myself with until my classmates finished. So I would use that week's work list to write a little story. And every week I'd write another story, and they began to fit together, and before long I couldn't wait for spelling lessons so that I could find out where the words would lead me. Through language an entire world opened up that I hadn't predetermined.

I am in Los Angeles on the eve of a poetry reading. Since I'd been told I would be put up in the Marriott, I didn't eat dinner before the trip; I would treat myself to room service, a long bath, then bed. But it's eight o'clock, and I'm in a motel with no restaurant attached. So I phone a pizza parlor for the calorie-rich meal I didn't intend. While waiting for the delivery I take out my notebook and write:

> This is the point in all the books where the hero pockets the hotel keys and sets out to explore the city. This is the point where he stumbles across a crime, or is accosted by the drunk eager to tell his life story. World literature is littered with scenes like this, the dark street streaked with neon and the sidewalks glinting with starlight and granite chips, the lone hero melancholy and intense under the stars.
>
> But I am a woman, and this is a motel with only exterior stairs—hence unprotected, hence dangerous.
>
> As a woman, I am forbidden nightwalks. I stand in my fenced yard

hanging up laundry half naked on an Arizonan summer night and scoot inside when I hear the gravel crunch in the alley.

This is energy I could be using elsewhere.

When I look out onto the landscape, I do <u>not</u> see the "fresh green breast" of the New World. I do not dream of overpowering it; I do not believe it will nurture, seduce, or satisfy me. But it will meet me halfway, so to speak. I do fantasize covering the territory . . . but with my feet, one ordinary tread after the other, my head suspended seven times its own length above all this activity—and I cover the distance with a clear intelligence and sound body, not with whispers and bedroom promises. And not with boots. I want to feel the pebbles under my foot.

———————————

By the end of February the goldfish have become another piece of the furniture. I feel sorry for them; we pay them such scant attention. They remind me of the urgings circling inside me, urgings occasionally nosing the surface, hungry and mute. During the course of a day we throw a few flakes onto the quivering membrane and hope they will filter down: notebooks clogged with scattered lines and grocery lists, notebooks thrown away in fury when the child finds them and, delightedly imitating Mommy, scribbles them full. Poems squeezed into a bright afternoon when she goes to the home of a classmate, silent thanks to that other mother. And of course, the reciprocal gesture, inviting one of her playmates home, deciding that this madcap visit is the perfect time for writing business letters, since letters can be easily and often interrupted. (They can also turn into computer salad.) Or ironing while making phone calls, so that chores won't cut into writing time, and then having to ask husband or child to massage out the neck-kinks later.

Many of these stratagems are most convenient; but what's insidious in this pattern is the guilt that emerges whenever I need to take a block of prime time for myself: Sit the child in front of two hours of videotaped *Sesame Street*s so that a poem can be written? Guilt.

Accept my husband's offer to stay at home while he takes our daughter to Kiwanis Park? Guilt. Hire a babysitter so I can write in my office at the university (only on weekends; otherwise students will knock to say: "How lucky to catch you here!")—in other words, farm my baby out? Guilt.

Goldfish, I've heard, will grow to fill the space they are put in. My study is compact, a converted child's bedroom, and the window looks out on the fenced-in yard but at chest level, so that when I sit down at the desk all I can see is the upper lip of the fence and the neighbors' palm tree. I chafe against this impediment even while realizing that most older ranch houses have windows like this. I want a second story, so that I can look down on the neighborhood— not in arrogance, but so that I have a clear and composed view. Of course, I'm lucky to have a room for myself, where no one disturbs the (dis)order of my desk.

For all the years of my self-reflective life, I have hankered for space molded to my liking, searching for rooms to personalize. Even part of a room: a dining-room tabletop polished to a dark sheen upon which to place my writing pad at 6 A.M. before Mom comes downstairs to fix Dad's breakfast, a cheap metal desk painted turquoise to look less sterile. When I was ten, a few months before my first period, I built an entire house in my mind, daydreaming through muggy summer afternoons, arms cocked behind my head on the chenille bedspread. It was a small house, one room fashioned of adobe block I would make myself, hacking clay from our backyard, mixing in water and straw, packing the goop in wooden forms and praying for drought so that they could dry evenly. This dream house would stand in the backyard, away from the house with its clinging odors but close enough to run back. . . just in case. It would be whitewashed inside and out, with no chairs—just a ledge along three walls, spread with thick red rugs and set with white candles, and burning myrrh, and an Aeolian harp singing in the doorway.

That final bastion of childhood lasted just one summer, but I have re-created that room wherever I have resided, Ireland, Oberlin, Berlin, Paris; whether in the bare little side room in Alabama which flooded mornings with filtered light from the pines or the white walls of the upstairs living room at Madison Village, one of a thousand Styrofoam apartment complexes in Arizona. Or the arched alcove in Jerusalem with a view across the Kidron Valley to the gold facade of Mount Zion; or my mellow tangerine-and-cream study in "Old Tempe," in our house made of concrete block.

After about six years in this study I find myself hankering for more space. I am sick of looking at this yard. I remember my resentment of a month back, confined in a motel room without the option of going for a walk after dark, deprived of the luxury of choosing a restaurant and eating alone. Can it be that even as one grows to fit the space one lives in, one cannot grow unless there's space to grow?

From the red notebook:

> *Dana has moved into her first house and is painting it white. Only the floors are darker, in deference to practicality; the carpet is a trim dove gray, the shadow of white. I don't tell Dana about my first dream house. But I wonder—how many women have the dream of both light <u>and</u> containment?*

March 24: Tamarra and I have a meeting with the printer at 9 A.M. I love the world of the printshop—there is a calm and order, an *adagio* sense of time that permits the appreciation, the *heft,* of each detail—the positioning of a comma, the measured appraisal of every letter and space, the sheer physical investment of setting a page of type. Isn't this how every writer imagines writing, setting down each letter with deliberate care, setting it to last, tamping it in?

The photographs, softened through the collotype process, look as if they had grown into the paper. And my poems are so elegant, so confidently genteel in their beds of Rives Heavyweight Buff, that I am abashed. Did I write these? And the paper so thick, the pages so large!

The director of Pyracantha Press lays out several sample packets of binding materials with exotic names and hair's-breadth variations in color and texture. Then endpapers. Then discussion of price. He suggests a working figure.

"Nobody will buy it for that price!" Tamarra blurts. "We aren't worth . . ." She stops, suddenly aware of the import of what we're both thinking.

"This isn't just another book," he replies. "Tamarra, how much would you charge for a single one of these images? Rita, how much time did you put into each word, each line? There are seven images and seven poems. And they've been set by hand and handprinted on fine paper and the bindings glued by hand and sewn by hand. How long have you worked on this book? How long have we worked on its conception, and now, the book?" Then, very gently: "This book is worth more than you can ever ask for it."

I'm waiting for the goldfish to die. But they keep on living and growing, not monstrous at all but burgeoning. Aviva continues to ignore them. My husband cleans out the bowl periodically and I find myself sitting by them at odd moments, lost to everything but their silent, open-mouthed appeals. What are they saying? I know I should be writing; but I keep on listening.

LIFE AT CLOSE RANGE

GRETEL
EHRLICH

It's June and soon we'll be moving cattle to the high mountain pastures. Already the first slanting rains have come—black arrows that come back up as green grass. At this time of year it can still snow, but ducks and shorebirds stop over on our little lake to rest before going on to the Arctic or Canada. As soon as the mountain meltwater comes down, I go to work irrigating 125 acres of hay meadows and on the way, because I always carry binoculars, I keep track of what's on the pond: godwits, terns, mallards, teal, sora rails, snipes, and phalaropes. Coyotes come to drink early in the morning, vying with bald and golden eagles for a prairie dog on the way. It's not only what I do see as I set irrigation water, but what I don't see in the way of animals and birds that counts—those hidden ones like bears, mountain lions, badgers, ermine, and snakes who I know are here too, but I can't always see.

A writer's imagination must be like that: filled not just with literal truths, but with the unseen, the unknown whose shy presence is felt. What's underneath the lake water, the sod-bound fields, the lid of my skull, I wonder?

Yesterday lightning ignited a ridge above our ranch and, as quickly, a boisterous rain squall put it out. Then the hail came, dancing, blanching the land. The isolated ranch my husband and I inhabit often seems otherwordly: mist spills on us sweeping everything from sight, then on rising, the green-breasted earth steams. Last night the moon was so bright a moth inside the house beat against the window, trying to get out, and in the morning, at almost the same place, I found a blue luna moth, big as my hand, trying to get in. A writer's life must be like those moths, beating down obstructions to get at truths.

Sometimes when strangers ask what I do, I say I write, but around here, they think I said "ride." I do both of course, because most ranchwork is done on horseback. Writing is thought of as being cerebral work, while ranching, which takes up a good deal of my time, is mostly physical. But I couldn't write if I didn't ride and I'd find fourteen-hour days in the saddle quite tedious if I didn't have writing to come home to. In fact, I often write—notepad balanced on saddlehorn—gathering cattle, and when I'm in my writing room, a separate building on a hill with a view of the sorting corrals, I often get up mid-sentence to fix a panel of fence or change an irrigation dam, or put a stray horse away. This whole business of dividing body and mind is ludicrous. After all, the breath that starts the song of a poem, or the symphony of a novel—the same breath that lifts me into the saddle—starts in the body, and at the same time, enlivens the mind.

Our ranch is thirty miles from the nearest grocery store, eighty miles from a movie theater, a hundred and fifty miles from an airport, yet I feel as if I were at the center of things, "in media res." Our ranch, and the entire ecosystem in which it lies, is my laboratory. Wherever I am on it, whatever I'm doing, I'm always thinking, remembering, feeling, observing, absorbing, and listening—to wasps eating ants, to the eddies of wind above oceans of pines, to the pond ducks fighting at breeding time, to the whir of nighthawks diving down. But it's a curious laboratory, one in which I don't do experiments on nature, but nature experiments with me. I'm a land steward, but it's the land that tells me what's right and what's wrong, and I have to learn to listen.

If you live in a place—any place, city or country—long enough and deeply enough you can learn anything, the dynamics and inter-connections that exist in every community, be it plant, human, or animal—you can learn what a writer needs to know. Here, as any-where, the search for ways of knowing is a great discipline, an ultimate freedom in which you will find the entire world opens to you. When I began writing full time, I asked a well-known essayist his advice and he said, "Write from the heart," which was another way of saying, you must see through to the heart of things.

These days I do that by getting down on my hands and knees—literally and figuratively—and inspecting life at close range. From monitoring grass plants, soil quality, insects, and animals, as well as the health of entire watersheds, I've learned to scrutinize and savor the constructs of language, the points at which ideas, ethics, and sensations meet or collide, the way the tone of a piece of writing—like muscle tone, or the ecotone of a landscape—moves smoothly or drops out from under my pen. From diving into the midst of other lives, in nature and in the human realm, working as nurturer, stu-dent, midwife, I've stumbled on the liberating sense of equality that exists everywhere and have been able to dismiss with great convic-tion the idiotic idea of human dominance over nature, and know it to be physically and intellectually absurd. With equality comes a sense of the holiness—sacred or secular—of every animate and inan-imate thing.

Writing, like being a good hand with a horse, requires wakeful-ness and a willingness to surrender. I try to burn away preconception and let what is actually here come in. Any act of writing is a medita-tion on existence. It implies stopping, breathing in and out. "Do not write more clearly than you can think," the physicist Niels Bohr said. The truth is hard; no false décor allowed.

Riding out across a six-thousand-acre mountain pasture becomes an ambulation of mind. The body of the horse carries me into imagery, and memory, and, like the wind, I try to hone what has registered in me as a precision, making every word count, every word a tiny truth in itself. Roping a calf, I have to think ahead as the coil spins out, but at the same time, stay agile, flexible, alive in the present so that I can take my dallies with speed and care and not lose a thumb. Both jobs—writing and cowboying—take up the whole mind and heart. Weather pushes me the way I push at internal barriers and, after a decade or so, both jobs work together like mortar and pestle, the one pulverizing the other into clarity.

There is no knowing what makes a writer, what ingredients have contributed. Was it the stories my very urban (and urbane) grandfather told me over and over? Was it the frustration of being almost silent during my young life which fed the need to communicate, albeit on my own terms? Was it my inordinate love of animals and books—the one love growing alongside the other that led me to this isolated, animal-rich place where the play of the mind and heart could take a far reach? It seems that any list of ingredients will do except deadness, frivolity, the refusal to enter silence and loneliness and listen to what is inside. A writer makes a pact with loneliness. It is her, or his, beach on which waves of desire, wild mind, speculation break. In my work, in my life, I am always moving toward and away from aloneness. To write is to refuse to cover up the rawness of being alive, of facing death.

Early in my life, maybe from reading D. H. Lawrence, I dedicated myself to "living fully," which included reading, keeping my standards high. To write and not read the best that has been written (and only the best; there's not time for anything less) is foolish. It's like a gardener putting in seeds where there is no ground. It is in the context of our ordinary, everyday lives that seeds germinate. In the larger sense, place ultimately becomes a mirror of mind.

In his notebooks, Henry James wrote: "The law of the artist is the terrible law of fructification, of fertilization, the law of acceptance of all experience, of all suffering, of all life, of all suggestion and sensation and illumination." Looking out the windows of my writing room at this moment, I see an elk carrying mist on his shoulders, drifting out of a canyon; a duck diving for food; a meadowlark alighting on a fence post, tilting his head back and singing after a June rain.

A good hand on a ranch requires vigilance, acute powers of observation, readiness to anticipate what might go wrong or what's coming next, a taste for recklessness, intuitive skills, patience, and what cowboys look for when they buy a horse: a lot of heart. Aspiring to those qualities as a rancher, I can only hope my writing will benefit as well.

THE PROVINCE OF
RADICAL SOLITUDE

CAROLYN
FORCHÉ

Anna Bassarova stands in a ring of thawed snow, stirring a trash-fire in an iron drum. As she pokes the flames with a stick her face flares, shriveled and intent, and sparks rise into the night along with pages of burning ash from the week's papers. She is speaking to me in nineteenth-century Slovak, a language I have since forgotten; her words rise with the burning news. A page peels away from the rest, an ashen page framed in brilliance. For a moment, the words are visible, even though the fire has destroyed them, so transparent has the page become.

She looks at me, and where her eyes should be there are small wild flames. The sparks from her fire hiss out among the stars and in thirty years appear again as red tracer rounds fired above Beirut airport. I recall standing transfixed at the sight of them, unable to move when the accompanying mortar fire struck the nearby hills. In that moment it seemed possible to discern a peculiar design in their trajectory from my grandmother's refuse-fire to the Shouf mountains of Lebanon. But by what design would the granddaughter of a Czechoslovak needle-maker have become a poet at all, much less one who would be asked her impressions of a war zone in the Middle East? It seems to me now that I have lived a most improbable life, one which by turns blesses and bewilders me. My perception of the duration between the sparks' rising and falling is not one of clocked time. It is as if they simply crossed the child's night sky and landed in the life of the woman she has somehow become. If Anna were alive, I would ask her how this happened, but as she is not, it is necessary for me to open my memory and consciousness, as the site of a rather difficult self-excavation.

The past leaves its residue of debris: the past itself, the world in pieces, which we fondly and in our bewilderment retrieve so as to make our meaning. We live in ruins then, which are by turns abandoned, inhabited, excavated, and destroyed. The shards of the past may be pieced together so as to comfort us with an illusion of commensurate memory. *It was like this,* we say, except that there were no pieces missing, and the cracks weren't visible.

If I were to mark particular fragments of my own journey, I would begin with Detroit, a city in ruin, and with its surrounding farmlands no longer farmed, in the period called "postwar." For the children of that era, the present was eternal and the future fictitiously invoked to overwhelm and obliterate the past, which was submerged in parental silence. Postwar American children were therefore vulnerable to being haunted by memories of experiences which we did not have. The world into which we were born was wounded, and particularly in America, the suture of choice for the closing of this wound was silence. We remembered always that we could not remember.

Childhood was the province of radical solitude. To Anna, it was an "American invention," an absurd cartoon offered as a preview of American life. She went nightly to make her fire, writing in the snow with her boots. I remember rubbing an opening into the steamed kitchen window in order to see her, tethered to the long blue trail of her bootprints. Her tracks were as "meaningful" as her language: uneven, obscure, inscribing absence. She never assimilated, and although she was "naturalized," never became more than a refugee from a country erased by war. Relatives who had remained behind in the occupied zone of her past sometimes sent letters, and after reading them she always wept. Her gift to me was an insistence that the world as I knew it was not the only world, and American life not the only possible life. The ranch houses going up around us, the shopping strips, the fields turned into developments were, in her word, "Nothing. You have nothing here," she said. "This is all nothing."

So I was left to imagine what something might be, and this is how my other life began: parallel to this one, in the narrative of a child who had herself been displaced. Everything that happened in the "real" world happened as well in the story, but in the latter there were greater richness and difficulty. Things were more precisely beheld: snow touching chopped wood, cake flour clinging to Anna's hair, a headless doll on fresh sheets. Fragments of speech were also gathered: "They did not want you to know the past. They were hoping in this way you could escape it." And: "Life is strange, *dushenka,* we none of us know what it is." I narrated in this manner into my seventeenth year, or rather, as long as a narrated identity was necessary and bearable. Sometimes this story corresponded to what I was "actually" doing, sometimes not. In my earliest journals, I now read a desire to see the world precisely but also fictively. In my earliest hand, the dogs lick sunlight from the walks, the wet paper of Anna's flesh drapes her bones, and horses hoove the snow pack. In the hospital, Anna vomits into the basin and cries They are making me worse. I hear this from the mouth of a feared and beloved woman, and later write it so that not only does she speak again, but despairs again of a life she has since lost.

Under the black locust trees in summer, my closest friend and I read our stacks of books, selected by Mrs. Nagy, the aging local librarian and bibliophile, who seemed to know exactly which nineteenth-century novels contained what she called "passages of purple prose." These she withheld from us, shelving them in the "adult section," which of course we read when her back was turned. Sometimes we performed the stories, acting them ourselves or with our dolls. On rainy days we read in an out-building on the Stamen farm in sweet hay among tools. Even then, we knew what we wanted. I would become a poet and one day live in Paris. Lois Dorando would become Lois Dorando de Caraminana and would live in Spain. By some lovely confluence of fate and desire, both of us reached our destinations precisely.

My voracious reading was encouraged by my mother, even though I hear her over and over in my memory calling out, "Will you put that book down now please and help?"

If reading was a pleasurable journey, often into a world more difficult than my own, writing was the tenuous thread I secreted, and from which I remained suspended. In this way I was able to catch myself (or be caught) in a reverberating web of words.

In the evenings Anna listened to Slovak radio programs of news, the Mass in Slovak, and accordian polkas. The lighted city of radio tubes was Slovakia. An Extreme Unction kit was kept in the linen closet, consisting of a hollowed crucifix holding beeswax candles, cotton swabs, and a glass vial of blessed oil, in the event someone died in the house. We were not to touch it. The house was inhabited by seven children, three adults, and ten guardian angels. A ghost lived in the long mirror in my mother's room. We were told never to cross picket lines or speak with strangers. The houses behind the field had no indoor toilets. They were tornado-ravaged, and built of rust-stained breeze-block and tar paper. Beside one of them rose a hill of empty liquor bottles. The children of that house were sometimes beaten, and in summer our open windows ushered in their screams. One of the boys had to have his leg amputated for a mysterious reason. The nearby lake was bottomless and always cold. I did chores after school, repetitive mindless labors, during which it was possible to cultivate an inner life. Whatever I happened to be doing, I was not there; however long I was alone there was something present, the one whom I addressed, variously and severally called God, the one not yet born or yet encountered, that which I was not, an unknown self. However the Other was apprehended, it called forth this address. This was not "magical thought." There was no sense of word conjuring Being. There was only the necessity of inner speech.

The presence of this Other filled the world. Objects at times appeared radiant, or as if illuminated from within. The world breathed and was awake. This was also the source of its terror, which remained ineffable for me until I read in Emmanuel Levinas:

> One sleeps alone, the adults continue life; the child feels the silence of his bedroom as "rumbling". . . . It is something resembling what one hears when one puts an empty shell close to the ear, as if the emptiness were full, as if the silence were a noise. It is something one can feel when one thinks that even if there were nothing, the fact that "there is" is undeniable. Not that there is this or that; but the very scene of being is open: there is. In the absolute emptiness that one can imagine before creation—there is.

This "there is" interrupted my solitude and made the world strange. Mirror, bed, curtain, all became strange. My own hands became someone else's. My sister also suffered from these episodes, later explained away as "anxiety attacks," and we employed various strategies to counteract or preempt them, until one day I discovered that the strangeness was interesting in itself. Even words could become strange, become detached from meaning. One could say *milk, milk, milk* until it became a guttural noise.

There is a word in Slovak and also in Russian: *ostrenenie,* which means the making strange of objects or persons. Years later, I discovered that Viktor Shklovsky and the Russian Formalists consciously

practiced *ostrenenie* as a technique, and believed that defamiliariza-
tion was the very task or work of art. I learned to do this as a child,
and also accommodated myself to its occurrence.

Before the open fields became "vacant lots" (available for construction), they were summery expanses of high grass, Queen Anne's
lace, horsetail, and cornflower smoothed by the winds, and we
waded through them as through waist-high water. It was possible to
lie down and disappear to all but whatever kept watch over the
earth. In such hours I felt myself become smaller. The stalks of fake
wheat filled with light, as did the wings of swallowtails and mon-
archs. The world hummed, and my own speech rose above the
humming and was measured by it. I didn't know what metered verse
was, but I remember knowing that language rose and fell, and that it
occurred most pleasurably in utterances of similar length. One could
recite for hours the flow of language in patterns. My early musical
and rhythmic training derived from the Latin liturgy, most especially from litany recitations and Gregorian plainsong. Rhythm,
however, is of the body, and it was during walks in childhood that I
first sensed the relation between breath, phrase, and heart. I spoke to
the pounding.

My school was a mile away down Powers Road, then a dirt
township road through the woods, lined with open ditches of cattail
and skunk cabbage. On cold days the little houses sent up pencil lines
of smoke. If I was made to wear boots or leggings, I hid them in an
empty culvert at the swamp's edge. When the wind rose or a truck
passed, the road was raised in a white cloud, and gravel ticked against
my legs. The road's length changed, depending upon whether or not
I was late, but usually I liked walking and the lightheadedness of
becoming winded. Sunlight broke the canopy of maple and oak. The
language came then in hard little pumping rhythms broken by
prayer or song. If a horse cantered toward me through ground fog, it
meant something. If the birds left the phone wires before I reached
them, something else. Sometimes I made little agreements with the

Other: if no trucks passed within the next forty steps, it was a sign that I would find a missing book. It was, then, possible to read the world by means of these signs. But mostly the walk enabled the story to pass through me uninterrupted.

When I was grown, I never remained in one place very long. I was counseled that my practice would conflict with work, which demands of most writers a settled and quiet exterior life, but I often wondered about the advice given to young writers: "Write about what you know." I understand this to mean that there is, even in the most limited of circumstances, a treasure of infinite richness, which, if not fixed (possessed as knowledge), may be explored through the word. Perhaps this advice is also a kind of epistemological koan. Is it possible to write otherwise? I think that, particularly in America, its buried message might be read as cautionary: "Don't go there. You already know enough." This seems to reinforce zones not to be transgressed by the American poet, located in the world "outside" the self: social, political, and historical zones.

Several times as a young woman I crossed the United States alone in a Volkswagen, and later went off into the rest of the world. I came to understand my life as a path: erased behind, meandering and invisible ahead. Anna was herself nomadic, disappearing for weeks or months only to reappear with yet more stories of Mennonites or Indians encountered in the hills of Pennsylvania or Ohio. I also knew that she had stowed away in the cargo hold of a ship at the age of nine, and spent two years at sea as a galley maid. She has gypsy in her, they said, the settled ones, who almost always expressed disapproval.

Psychiatrists, politicians, tyrants are forever assuring us that the wandering life is an aberrant form of behaviour; a neurosis; a form of unfulfilled sexual longing; a sickness which, in the interests of civilisation, must be suppressed. Nazi propagandists claimed that gypsies and Jews—peoples with wandering in their genes—could find no place in

THE PROVINCE OF RADICAL SOLITUDE

a stable Reich. Yet, in the East, they still preserve the once universal concept: that wandering re-establishes the original harmony which once existed between man and the universe. [Bruce Chatwin, from *The Songlines*]

My mother's impulse was to protect our childhoods from intrusion. On the matter of evil in the world, she invoked silence and spiritual grace. It is my present judgment that Anna felt little but contempt for this protection. She preferred to address ourselves-to-come, our future selves, in a language we would decipher when we were grown. We were alive, she reasoned, and therefore not too young for life. These two women in their separate ways gifted me with a sense of estrangement. I lived through books, physical labor, and reverie. It was not, of course, until I was grown that I appreciated my difference as a blessing.

Some of my schoolmates were less fortunate. As the cathode ray structured the consciousness of postwar American children, the invention of childhood sequestered us in a temporal sphere of wonder, enchantment, and vacuity. The world was re-created through animation: the ordinary terrors of the forming mind were reflected in caricatures of animals and people enduring simulated violence with no sense of consequence. Images replaced images in such rapid succession that sustained contemplation and engagement were not only impossible but unnecessary. With the passage of time, this condition has only become more pronounced. In technological time, space is compressed and we inhabit a smaller world in which the velocity of experiential time has been increasing. Are there not regions of consciousness inaccessible at these speeds?

We are beginning to appreciate the destructive effects of our so-called progress upon an environment which we mysteriously persist in objectifying as somehow removed or separate from ourselves. But we have not yet begun to address how this destruction has altered us. Perhaps certain forms of human consciousness can also become extinct. The unthinkable was once a euphemism for annihilation. Now that we are adjusted to thinking through and beyond this subject, perhaps the unthinkable can refer to all that can no longer be thought. If "Every epoch dreams its successor" (*Chaque époque rêve la suivante*), what is ours dreaming?

The Holocaust (or Shoah) was once unthinkable, and its occurrence has been said to have "ruptured" history: to have, that is, interrupted it, provoking Theodor Adorno to wonder if writing poetry "after the Holocaust" wasn't itself "barbaric." Adorno's objection to poetry after the Holocaust echoes Walter Benjamin's insistence that "there is no document of civilization which is not at the same time a document of barbarism." After the Holocaust or annihilation, no poem can avoid the implication of its actuality as one more cultural document, though perhaps (as Benjamin suggests) it can "brush history against the grain."

The question now is whether one can think of this period as post-Holocaust at all. The paradigm is still operative. Czeslaw Milosz says, "If a thing exists in one place, it will exist everywhere." Without losing sight of the historical specificity of the Shoah, we can say that its thinking continues in the technology of mass annihilation. Our weapons, if deployed, would destroy the material and spiritual worlds on behalf of the ideological. Holocaust thinking also continues as participation in environmental destruction against organic and inorganic forms which are first distanced through objectification (in order, for example, to be known) and, once possessed, rendered subordinate even unto their elimination.

We busy ourselves standardizing measurements and procedures, rendering languages, modes of inquiry, and even pedagogy computer-compatible in our quest for an abstract universality, which harbors within it a desire for the elimination of difference. Women may understand this to include their own otherness. This process—which perfects by elimination—has also affected other life forms (with the extinction of half the earth's known species predicted by the year 2000), and it has certainly affected our own. If we fail to see this as a war against variation, multiplicity, and plurality, it isn't difficult to guess its fulfillment.

It is possible to practice meeting the world, rather than regarding it as an object of knowledge, to leave behind the desire to appropriate experience, and begin to think in terms of relation. Levinas says that ethics is a response to the face of a stranger that "*summons me, questions me, stirs me, provokes my response or my responsibility.*" This stranger is anyone *other* than ourselves. We don't write "about" the Other or another, purporting to capture, describe, render, or represent Otherness. We write out of our encounter and out of our being marked by it.

To enter into relation, not only with the world but with one's work, it is necessary to let go of the desire to have experiences; one does not journey, labor, love, or even read in order to have them. Experience as such occurs within the self, and whatever it is, it is only of the self, and not of the world. When the world is regarded as an object of knowledge or a source of experience, the meeting is not with one's full being. Part of one's being is "having" experience or "learning" the world.

In conditions of extremity (war, suffering, struggle), the witness in relation cannot remove him- or herself. Relation is proximity, and this closeness subjects the witness to the possibility of being wounded. No special protection can be sought and no outcome intended. The witness who writes out of extremity writes his or her wound, as if such writing were making an incision. Consciousness itself is cut open. The self is fragmented, and the vessel of self breaks into shards. These may be pieced together, but the cracks remain visible. The narrative also breaks. At the site of the wound, language breaks, interrogates itself, becomes tentative, kaleidoscopic. The form of this language bears the trace of extremity, and is often composed of fragments: questions, aphorisms, broken passages of lyric prose or poetry, quotations, bits of memory and dialogue, brief and lucid passages resembling what the voice recognizes as its former work.

For three years after my return from El Salvador (in 1980), I did not write. My practice had been to wait in meditative expectancy before the page, and to begin writing with whatever was released when my pen touched paper. I sometimes imagined that words coursed into my fingers between poems, and even, at times, felt their presence as a slight cramp or pain. My only rule for myself had been never to begin by knowing what I was going to write: to begin without intention. This requires, however, a quieting of the will, and the will, of course, becomes more insistent with the passage of unproductive time. For a while, I was confused about my empty-handedness. Regardless of the reason, the page remained white.

Between 1981 and 1986, I traveled to Belfast, Mexico City, Costa Rica, New York, Beirut, Tokyo, Hiroshima, Nagasaki, Nairobi, Johannesburg, and Paris. During this time I wrote, filling many hundreds of pages with what I thought of as "notes" in the best of moments, and failed poems in the worst. An assortment of odd little notebooks was also filled. In early 1987, I despaired of writing again. For seven years I had produced essays, reviews, and radio programs, had been interviewed, critiqued, read and misread, and both celebrated and castigated almost always for extra-literary reasons—but I had not written, or rather, what I was writing was unrecognizably mine.

In April of that year, while living in a rented house in Province-town, Massachusetts, on the bay side, my "angel" appeared. For two hours a day, a friend came to take my baby son, and I was left in solitude again before the page, this time almost recklessly free of concern for what would emerge. Every day I received five pages from my hands, with two hours passing. The work didn't resemble, I thought, anything I'd ever done. The lines were long and at times almost aphoristic. "I" seemed to be several rather than one. My English would suddenly break into French, and even once a little

German song insisted to be sung. After a few days, I knew the very moment when my friend would open the little gate and bring my boy back to me. I couldn't see the gate, but it had been five pages. Once or twice, at the end of the two hours, I felt tears running down my face. Someone had been crying the poem to the page. Or was I relieved? One day I realized that this work was very like the earlier "notes."

I had a little sign in my kitchen then: "Whatever keeps you from doing your work has become your work." This was to encourage me to understand that if I were going to write poetry, I could not expect from myself immaculate closets. But now I read the sign in a new way. This strange, broken, fragmented, and flaring language was what I now had to write. Within a month or two, I knew that it was a long, experimental work in sequences, many-voiced because of my own brokenness. I also realized that I had been making this work for many years, and that it was, in a sense, also a response to Walter Benjamin's desire that just such a writing be attempted. As an *hommage* to him, the work will be titled *The Angel of History*.

Now it is three years, and the manuscript is in its last months. *Angel* is not "about" experiences. It is for me the opening of a wound, the muffling and silence of those seven years, and it is also a gathering of utterances that have lifted away from the earth and wrapped our weather in risen words, some of which were, perhaps, Anna's. These utterances issue from my own encounter with events of my century, but do not represent "it." The first-person free verse lyric-narrative poem ·of my earlier years has given way to a work which has desired its own bodying forth: broken, haunted, and in ruins, with no possibility of restoration.

WRITING WITH THE BODY

LUISA VALENZUELA

As I leave the ambassador's residence in Buenos Aires early one morning in 1977, at the height of my country's military dictatorship, and walk through the dark, tree-lined streets, I think I am being followed. I have been hearing political testimony from people who sought asylum in the Mexican embassy. Enemies of the de facto government. I think that I can be abducted at any moment. Yet I feel immensely vital, filled with an inexplicable strength that may come from my having reached some kind of understanding. I walk back home through those streets that appear to be empty, and take all the precautions I can to make sure that I'm not being followed, that I'm not being aimed at from some doorway, and I feel alive. I would say happy.

Now I know why.

The answer is simple, now, so many years later. I felt—at this moment, I feel—happy because I was—am—writing with the body. Writing that lingers in the memory of my pores. Writing with the body? Yes. I am aware of having done this throughout my life, at intervals, although it may be almost impossible for me to describe. I'm afraid that it's a matter of a secret action or a mode of being that may be ineffable.

But I don't believe in the ineffable. The struggle of every person who writes, of every true writer, is primarily against the demon of that which resists being put into words. It is a struggle that spreads like an oil stain. Often, to surrender to the difficulty is to triumph, because the best text can sometimes be the one that allows words to have their own liberty.

While writing with the body one also works with words, sometimes completely formed in one's mind, sometimes barely suggested. Writing with the body has nothing to do with "body language." It implies being fully committed to an act which is, in essence, a literary act.

At the Mexican embassy that night in 1977, I had just spoken at length with an ex-president who was a political refugee, as well as with a terrorist who had also sought asylum. Both men were sitting at the same table; we were all somewhat drunk and, because of that, more sincere. Then I walked down the streets and as I was walking, I was writing with the body. And not just because of a letter that I was mentally addressing to my friend, Julio Cortázar. I was telling him in the letter—because I knew that I was risking my life and was afraid—that I don't want to play "duck": when I get into the water, I choose to get wet.

I was writing with the body, and fear had much to do with this. Fear.

I was the kind of child who always poked around wherever there was fear: to see what kind of a creature fear was. I played at being a snake, a snail, or a hippopotamus in a warm African river. Among the animals I avoided was the ostrich. I wanted nothing to do with hiding my head in the sand. I don't know what crazy, morbid impulse made me run through the dark long hallways to the foyer at the entrance of my house, in the middle of the night, when the clock—controlled by witches—struck the hour. Nor do I know what made me go to the terrace where there was supposed to be a two-headed eagle, or behind the house where all kinds of dangers were lurking. I would have preferred hiding my head under the covers. But then who would reassure me? How could my eyes face daylight if they couldn't face shadows in the night? This is why I would go to look, and maybe because I looked came the need, sometime much later, to tell what I had seen.

Why?

Because of surprise

Because of adventure

Because of a question, and a gut rejection of any answers.

You tend to ask yourself why write with your entire body when you have that simple upper extremity which, thanks to the evolution of the species, has an opposable thumb especially made for holding a pen.

You also ask yourself—and this is really overwhelming—why write at all? In my case, I belong, body and soul and mind, to the so-called Third World where certain needs exist that are not at all literary.

Then other responses (or perhaps they are excuses) come to mind. The need to preserve collective memory is undoubtedly one of them.

There is yet another good excuse: writing as one's destined vocation. But I don't know if literature was my destiny. I wanted to be a physicist, or a mathematician, and, before that, an archaeologist or anthropologist, and for a long time I wanted to be a painter. Because I was raised in a house full of writers and that wasn't for me. No, ma'am. No thanks.

Fernando Alegría now describes that moment and place as the Buenos Aires Bloomsbury and this description isn't as crazy as it may appear. In our old house in the Belgrano section of town, the habitués were named Borges, Sábato, Mallea. My mother, the writer

Luisa Mercedes Levinson, was the most sociable person in the world when she wasn't in bed, writing.

When I was a child, I would look from the door of her room and she would be in her bed surrounded by papers, all day until sunset when the others arrived. I would watch her with admiration and with the conviction that that life wasn't for me. I wanted a different future.

Disguises I chose for Carnivals:

Aviatrix

Woman Explorer

Robin Hood

Those were the masks that belonged to the official Carnival. But other masks at other times also took the shape of exploration and adventure. I would climb onto the roofs of the neighboring houses to try and reach the end of the block, something which was impossible to do because of the gardens in between. On those days when I felt really daring, I would climb up to a stone angel that clung to a column and that needed my presence, because otherwise no one would ever see it. I would also sneak into empty lots, or explore an abandoned house around the block. I was always looking for treasures that changed according to my ambitions: colorful figurines, stamps, coins. There was an old guard at the abandoned house who would let us in and was our friend. Until one afternoon, after exploring the basement looking for secret passages—at that time we pretended that the house belonged to German spies or was it a smuggler's hideout?—the old guard greeted us with his fly open and all those strange things hanging out. I ran away with my best friend in tow. I never went back, but years, thousands of years later, I wondered if that was the treasure for which we searched.

Now I know: with that small adventure around the block and with those big stories I made up, I began the slow learning process of writing with the body

Because

pores or ink, it is the same thing

the same stakes.

Clarice Lispector knew it and in her books focused on that love-hate, that happiness-misfortune we call literature. Her novels appear to be about love and the search for knowledge but they are also different ways of speaking about writing.

One's happiness is greatest when the story flows like a stream of clear water, even if the worst abominations are being narrated. It is only during the reading of those passages that the fear of what has flowed from one's own pen takes over.

There is another misfortune in writing and it is perhaps the most painful. It is inscribed during times of silence, when nothing is written with the body or mind or hand. Periods of drought which seem to be of nonexistence.

This is why I say sometimes that writing is a full-time curse.

I also say that, in its best moments, writing a novel is a euphoric feeling, like being in love.

And to think that my mother, the writer, is to blame for all of this. Not because of the example she set, nor because of my emulation of her, which I acknowledge. She is to blame because when I was in the sixth grade in elementary school, my teacher asked her to help me with my compositions. "Your daughter is so bright in science," my teacher told her, "it's a shame that her grade should go down because she can't write." So my mother, overzealous in trying to help me, wrote a composition as she thought a tender eleven-year-old would.

I didn't think it was a very dignified text. From that moment on, I decided to assume the responsibility of my own writings. And that's how things are.

Because writing is the path that leads to the unknown. The way back is made of reflection, trying to come to terms with yourself and with that which has been produced. I strongly believe in the fluctu-

ation from intuition to understanding. Placing ourselves right there
  at the border
  between two currents
  at the center of the whirlpool,
  the eye of the tornado?

"You are too intelligent to be beautiful" is what many of us have
been told at some time by a man we've loved. Or, supposing literature is your profession: "You are too intelligent to be a good
writer." Contrasting, of course, that ugly, masculine thing which is
intelligence with female intuition. You wouldn't tell that to Susan
Sontag is what someone with clearer ideas would reply. But those
marks were made on young and tender skin, and from that moment
on, one will always have a feeling of inadequacy.

Incapable, inactive, unproductive. I think all of us, from the time
we're very young, feel at some time what could be called a nostalgia
for imprisonment: the crazy, romantic fantasy that a prisoner has all
the time to herself, to write. Only later do we realize that writing is
an exercise of liberty.

From exigencies and from temptations, the stuff of literature is
made. And from reflection, also. From everything. There is no un-
worthy material, although a great deal must be discarded.

When I was seventeen years old, I started working in journalism.
For many years it was the perfect combination, one that allowed me
to be part of all the disciplines, to go everywhere, and, at the same
time, to write. A gift of ubiquity wrapped in words. I had the
tremendous luck, almost a miracle, of having a boss who was a true
teacher. Ambrosio Vencino was not a journalist; he was a displaced
man of letters. To him I owe my obsessive precision with language.

I owe my travels to myself, to my need to touch the world with
my own hands. I never paid attention to the premise that you don't
have to leave your own bedroom to know the world. I traveled, I
continue traveling, and I sometimes think that in all those displace-
ments, parts of my self are being left behind.

Rodolfo Walsh, the Argentine writer and activist, once told me when I was complaining about how much I went from one place to the next and how little I wrote: "Your writing is also made from your travels."

Many years later, my writing was also made from another of Rodolfo Walsh's lessons to which I didn't pay much attention at the time. One day he showed me the difficult physical exercises that Cuban guerrillas practiced then in the Sierra Maestra. That physical guerrilla wisdom seemed to stand me in good stead in 1975 and 1976, when I sat in the cafes of Buenos Aires, devastated by state terrorism, and wrote stories that were, in a way, guerrilla exercises.

I put my body where my words are.

The physical loss hasn't been as great for me as it has been for others. I haven't been tortured, beaten, or persecuted. Knock on wood. I've been spared, perhaps because my statements aren't frontal; they are visions from the corner of my eye, oblique. I think we must continue writing about the horrors so that memory isn't lost and history won't repeat itself.

As a teenager, I was a voracious reader and I bragged about it but there were two books that I read in secret: *Freud* by Emil Ludwig and *The Devil in the Flesh* (*Le Diable au Corps*) by Raymond Radiguet. With these two books I may not have gone very far in terms of pornographic material but it's clear that my libido was already acting up.

That writing with the body known as the act of love happened later, as it should have, and turned out quite well, with great style, but with more of an inclination toward the short story than the novel.

I love the short story for being round, suggestive, insinuating, microcosmic. The story has both the inconvenience and the fascination of new beginnings.

The novel, on the other hand, requires more concentration, more time, a state of grace. I love it because of the joy in opening new paths as words progress.

Paths to the unknown, the only interesting ones.

What I already know bores me, makes me repetitive. This is why whenever I have had a good plot that was clearly thought out, I was forced to give it up or at least to compress it, trying to squeeze out the juice that wasn't visible at first sight.

If I had to write my creed, I would first mention humor:

I believe in having a sense of humor at all costs

I believe in sharp, black humor

I believe in the absurd

in the grotesque

in everything which allows us to move beyond our limited thinking, beyond self-censorship and the censorship by others, which tends to be much more lethal. Taking a step to one side to observe the action as it is happening. A necessary step so that the vision of political reality is not contaminated by dogmas or messages.

I have nothing to say.

With luck, something will be said through me, despite myself, and I might not even realize it.

It is said that women's literature is made of questions.

I say that women's literature consequently is much more realistic.

Questions, uncertainties, searches, contradictions.

Everything is fused, and sometimes confused, and implicates us. The true act of writing with the body implies being fully involved. I am my own bet; I play myself, as though lying on the roulette table, calling out "All or nothing!"

What is interesting about the literary wager is that we do wager everything, but we don't know against what.

They say that women's literature is made of fragments.

I repeat that it is a matter of realism.

It is made of rips, shreds of your own skin which adhere to the paper but are not always read or even legible. Shreds that can be of laughter, of sheer delight.

Sometimes while writing, I have to get up to dance, to celebrate the flow of energy transforming itself into words. Sometimes the energy becomes words that are not printed, not even with the delicate line of a fountain pen, which is the most voluptuous in the act of writing. You must always celebrate when—whether in a cafe or subway—a happy combination of words, a fortuitous allusion, elicits associations that unwind the mental thread of writing without a mark. The mark comes next. And I will do my best to retain the freshness of that first moment of awe and transformation.

Translated from the Spanish
by Cynthia Ventura and Janet Sternburg

WHITE LANTERNS

DIANE ACKERMAN

I

For the past week, I have been sailing around Antarctica, a landscape as scintillatingly sensuous as it is remote, whose crystal desert I've wanted to see for so long. Some months ago, I helped to raise baby penguins in quarantine at Sea World in San Diego. One fluffy, brown, Yeti-shaped, painfully adorable chick, which I became particularly close to, I named "Apsley," after Apsley Cherry-Gerrard who, in 1911, trekked across Antarctica, and later wrote a vivid and beguiling book about it, *The Worst Journey in the World.* For the last two years, I've been writing natural history essays for *The New Yorker,* which has sent me here to see and write about penguins in the wild.

Although my days are full of astonishing vistas, and lots of activity—climbing tussock-covered hills, exploring abandoned whaling stations, strolling among penguin rookeries—I've brought with me miscellaneous writerly odd jobs to work on in vacant moments. There are letters to answer, books to read, a couple of unrequited poems to finish, and notes for an essay on poetry. When I was reorganizing my files at home last week, I happened on one labeled "Science, Technology and Society," an interdisciplinary department at Cornell, whose weekly philosophical seminars I attended when I was a graduate student. I was a twenty-two-year-old poet then; prose was an unknown and frightening terrain, and I hadn't yet learned how to think comfortably in it. Nor to think comfortably at all. I had *a good mind,* as they say, but it was completely untrained. I learned little as an undergraduate at Penn State, except where things were located. Certainly I didn't learn to love knowledge or feel called by literature. A student there was obliged to take *either* Shakespeare or Milton. And the writing courses I took were mainly a sham. I remember how one writing professor, on the first day of class, gave us a long list of what he would not allow us to write. Graduate school was by no means the obvious choice for me.

I had wanted to write books while I did anthropological work somewhere in a jungle or on a veldt, but I ended up making a very difficult choice among three possible paths: going to Tanzania, to help with chimpanzee research at Jane Goodall's site; digging up earthquake victims in Peru; graduate work in an M.F.A. program. Cornell offered me a Teaching Assistantship, financial support, and two years in which to write. Even though I desperately wanted to see the world and be out in nature, I wanted even more to perfect myself as a writer. So, after much agonizing and soul-searching, I decided on graduate school, and, looking back, it was as if someone then threw a switch in my life, which suddenly began going in a different direction.

When I arrived at Cornell, I was badly educated, couldn't write prose, and didn't have a trained mind. But I did have a lot of curiosity, a somewhat eccentric and swervy imagination, and what seemed to me then almost limitless mental energy. One day I was listening to Gustav Holst's *The Planets,* and I thought how sad it was that people needed to turn the planet Mars into a war god or the planet Venus into a femme fatale in order to appreciate them. I was reading general science books and magazines for fun; and the real planets, with their bizarre atmospheres and mysterious terrains, fascinated me. So, as I began planning a book-length suite of poems based on the science of the planets, I applied to Science, Technology and Society for support, and was thrilled to receive it. I joined a strange interdisciplinary seminar, which met to discuss awkward problems in biomedical ethics and other topics related mainly to science, ethics, and society. It was a seminar by invitation only, and each year it included faculty from different departments, and a couple of graduate students like myself who received fellowships.

While I was there, the other seminar members were always from philosophy or the sciences, and I often felt that I was the token creative person in their midst. My natural urge was to solve the problems we were discussing. I wanted to come up with a list of workable solutions, choose the best one, and act on it. This amused them no end. Rather than calling me a writer, they referred to me as a "primary agent," by which they meant that, like a painter or composer, I *did* things, while they, on the other hand, discussed things. I often arrived fresh from the stable, carrying purple riding chaps and smelling of things earthier, to discuss such thorny subjects as euthanasia, which we were on no account to make up our minds about or to try to resolve in any practical way. But I learned a lot about how other sensibilities worked. I enjoyed thinking about difficult moral issues. I wasn't trained in the dressage of syllogistic argument, and ideas that I offered simply, thoughtfully, and from personal experience, without benefit of philosophical rhetoric, were often dismissed as amusing and well meant, but amateurish. We each had a brief, lunchtime seminar topic, and the one they assigned me was: "Is There Truth in Poetry?" Now, almost twenty years and seven books later, that topic haunts me again, this time in Antarctica.

II

Poetry is not philosophy, not sociology, not psychology, not politics. One ought not to ask of it what's found to better advantage elsewhere. One should only ask poetry to do what it excells at: (1) reflect the working sensibility of its creator, ideally someone with a unique vision and a unique way of expressing it, (2) remind us of the truths about life and human nature that we knew all along, but forgot somehow because they weren't yet in memorable language, and (3) reveal to us many incidental things that a poem knows so well.

What does a poem know? For openers, it knows the vagaries of linguistic fashion, the arduous, ricochet, and sometimes fanciful evolution of society as reflected in its language. It knows quite a lot about social convention, mob psychology, and mores, as they surface in the euphemisms of twenty ages—words like "lynch," "bloomers," and "fornicate"—and then submerge into normal discourse. A poem knows about Creation, any creation, our creation. It takes a blank and makes something, adds *some thing* to the sum of existence. If a poet describes a panther's cage in a certain vivid way, that cage will be as real a fact as the sun. A poem knows more about human nature than its writer does, because a poem is often a camera, a logbook, an annal, not an interpreter. A poem says: These are the facts. And sometimes it goes on to say: And this is what I make of them. But the facts may be right, and the *what I make of them* hopelessly wrong, in what is nonetheless a meaningful and moving poem. A poem may know the subtlest elisions of feeling, the earliest signs of some pattern or discord. It's only when we encounter Keats's odes as a set that we see budding in the first ones what will openly haunt the last. A book of poems chronicles the poet's many selves, and as such knows more about the poet than the poet does at any given time, including the time when the book is finished and yet another self holds her book of previous selves in her hands. A poem knows a great deal about our mental habits, and about upheaval and discovery, loneliness and despair. And it knows the handrails a mind clings to in times of stress (for Shelley, "veils"; for Rilke, "angels"; for Thomas, "wax").

A poem tells us about the subtleties of mood for which we have no labels. The voluptuousness of waiting, for instance: how one's whole body can rock from the heavy pounding of the heart. It knows extremes of consciousness, knows what the landscape of imagination looks like when the mind is at full-throttle, or beclouded, or cyclone-torn. Especially it tells us about our human need to make treaties. Often a poem is where an emotional or metaphysical truce takes place. Time slow-gaits enough in the hewing of the poem to make a treaty that will endure, in print, until the poet disowns it, perhaps in a second treaty called a "palinode." A poem knows about illusion and magic, how to glorify what is not glorious, how to bankrupt what is. It displays, in its alchemy of mind, the transmuting of the commonplace into golden saliences. It takes two pedestrian items, claps them together, and comes out with something finer than either one, makes them unite in a metaphor's common cause. A good example is Shelley's "the intense inane," where each humdrum word is elevated by the other. A poem records emotions and moods that lie beyond normal language, that can only be patched together and hinted at metaphorically. It knows about spunk, zealousness, obstinacy, and deliverance. It *accretes* life, which is why different people can read different things in the same poem. It freezes life, too, yanks a bit out of life's turbulent stream, and holds it up squirming for view, framed by the white margins of the page. Poetry is an act of distillation. It takes contingency samples, is selective. It telescopes time. It focuses what most often floods past us in a polite blur.

We expect the poet to be a monger of intensity, to pain for us, to reach into the campfire so that, like cautious Girl Scouts, we can linger in the woods and watch without burning ourselves or grubbying up our uniforms. Then, even if we don't feel the fire, we can see the poet's face illuminated by the light, hear her flushed chatter, the blazing wood crackle, and imagine well enough what the fire feels like from our safe remove. Though one can't live at red-alert from day to day, we expect the poet to, on our behalf, and to share that intensity with us when we're in the right mood. And if we become frightened or bored, we can simply put the poem back on the shelf. Really, we are asking the poet to live an extravagantly emotional life for us, so we can add her experiences to our own.

We read poems in part, I think, because they are an elegant, persuasive form of lying that can glorify a human condition feared to be meaningless, a universe feared to be "an unloving crock of shit," as philosopher Henry Finch once said off-handedly. To make physical the mystery is in some sense to domesticate it. We ask the poet to take what surpasses our understanding and force it into the straitjacket of language, to rinse the incomprehensible as free of telltale ambiguity and absurdity as possible. That's not to say that we don't find nature ambiguous or life absurd, only that the temptation to play and land the mystery like a slippery salmon, to freeze it in vocabularic aspic, is irresistible. Surely this is not far afield from the hunting magic of the cave drawings at Lascaux.

We ask the poet to reassure us by giving us a geometry of living, in which all things add up and cohere, to tell us how things buttress one another, circle round and intermelt. Once the poet has broken life into shards, we ask her to spin around and piece it back together again, making life seem even more fluid than before. Now it is a fluency of particulars instead of a nebulous surging. We ask the poet to compress and abbreviate the chaos, so we don't overload from its waterfall of sensations, all of which we nonetheless wish to some-how take in. There's more protein in a tiny piece of steak than in a whole loaf of bread, more food for thought in a line of Donne's than in a sermon (unless it's a sermon of Donne's). Because a poem tells us about the peculiar sensibility of the poet, it has a truth of structure, even when not of content. The poet records the fact of her mortality, though not always as straightforwardly or elegantly as Dylan Thomas does in the "Prologue" to his *Collected Poems:*

> I hack
> This rumpus of shapes
> For you to know
> How I, a spinning man,
> Glory also this star. . . .

The best poems are rich with observational truths. Above all, we ask the poet to teach us a way of seeing, lest one spend a lifetime on this planet without noticing how green light flares up as the setting sun rolls under, or the gauzy spread of the Milky Way on a star-loaded summer night, or what Beckett in *How It Is* calls "the fragility of euphoria among the sponges." The poet refuses to let things merge, lie low, succumb to visual habit. Instead she hoists things out of their routine, and lays them out on a white papery beach to be fumbled and explored. I don't mean to suggest that the subject of a poem is an end in itself. What it usually is is an occasion, catalyst, or tripwire that permits the poet to reach into herself and haul up whatever nugget of the human condition distracts her at the moment, something that can't be reached in any other way. It's a kind of catapult into another metaphysical county where one has longer conceptual arms. The poet reminds us that life's seductive habits of thought and sight can be broken at will. We ask the poet to shepherd us telescopically and microscopically through many perspectives, to lead us like a mountain goat through the hidden, multidimensionality of almost everything.

We expect the poet to know about a lot of strange things, to babysit for us, to help us relocate emotionally, to act as a messenger in affairs of the heart, to provide us with an intellectual calling card, to give us death's dumb show and escape's nimbus. Poetry is a kind of knowing, a way of looking at the ordinary until it becomes special and the exceptional until it becomes commonplace. It both amplifies and reduces experience, paradoxical though that be, shrinks an event teeming with disorder to the rigorous pungency of an epigram, or elasticizes one's perspective until, to use an image of Donne's, a drop of blood sucked by a single flea can accommodate an entire world order. Was abstraction ever so particular, so localized as it is in Donne? Or so orchestral a single glint as it is, say, in Milton's cosmological eye? "Milton's delight," notes Dr. Johnson, "was to sport in the wide regions of possibility; reality was a scene too narrow for his mind." Milton could say "All Hell broke loose" because he knew where (and what) Hell was; he had sent his wife and daughters there often enough, and his vision encompassed it, just as it did the constellations (many of which he introduces into *Paradise Lost*). He could say "Orion rose arm'd" because he'd observed Orion often enough when the arms weren't visible.

Poetry is a kind of attentiveness that permits one both the organized adventure of the nomad and the armchair security of the bank teller, a way of dabbling without being a dilettante. But poems ought not to be looked to as harbors of Truth, or poets as wardens of what is right.

III

Poetry was all I knew at twenty-one. So, it was also the only way I could know the All. Since then, I've struggled to learn to write prose, which doesn't come naturally to me, and was a nightmare chore for years. Now I find it comfortable, fascinating, sometimes even thrilling to write. My muse has become highly miscellaneous. Tomorrow, when we drift through the iceberg gardens of Gerlache Strait, I will be working—that is, writing prose. My mind will become a cyclone of intense alertness, in which details present themselves slowly, thoroughly, one at a time. I don't know how to describe what happens to me when I'm out in nature and "work-ing"—it's a kind of rapture—but it's happened often enough that I know to expect it. I've been wondering about the little penguin, Apsley, I grew close to at Sea World. Soon he will have fledged, replacing his thick brown down with black and white feathers, and look very different. My plan is to gather some pebbles from the rookery at Salisbury Plain, on South Georgia (where the egg he hatched from was collected), and take them back to him as a souve-nir. My souvenirs will, I hope, be some poems about Antarctica, perhaps spoken by the continent itself. Pebbles of another sort. Among the many kinds of nests writers create for the feathered mysteries that live inside them, I find poems more like nesting stones, and prose more like woven mud-and-twig nests. But both are home. I'm tempted to write a whole book of Antarctic poems, called *The White Lantern.* One astronaut, returning from space, said that he saw "a white lantern" glowing at the bottom of the world. That's just the right sort of radiant image to fuel a poet's thoughts.

THE WRITER ON, AND AT, HER WORK

URSULA K. LE GUIN

Her work
is never done.
She has been told that
and observed it for herself.
　　Her work
spins unrelated filaments
into a skein: the whorl
or wheel turns the cloudy mass
into one strong thread,
over, and over, and over.
　　Her work
weaves unrelated elements
into a pattern: the shuttle
thrown across the warp
makes roses, mazes, lightning,
over, and over, and over.

Her work
brings out of dirt and water
a whole thing, a hole where
the use of the pot is,
a container for the thing
contained, a holy thing, a holder,
a saver,
happening on the clayey wheel
between her and her clayey hands,
over, and over, and over.
Her work
is with pots and baskets,
bags, cans, boxes, carryalls,
pans, jars, pitchers, cupboards, closets,
rooms, rooms in houses, doors,
desks in the rooms in the houses,
drawers and pigeonholes in the desks,
secret compartments
in which lie for generations
secret letters.
Her work
is with letters,
with secret letters.
Letters that were not written
for generations.
She must write them
over, and over, and over.

She works with her body,
a day-laborer.
She labors, she travails,
sweating and complaining.

She is her instrument,
whorl, shuttle, wheel.
She is the greasy wool and the raw clay
and the wise hands
that work by day
for the wages of the worker.

She works within her body,
a night creature.
She runs between the walls.
She is hunted down and eaten.
She prowls, pounces, kills, devours.
She flies on soundless wings.
Her eyes comprehend the darkness.
The tracks she leaves are bloody,
and at her scream
everything holds still,
hearing that other wisdom.

Some say any woman working
is a warrior.
I resist that definition.
A fighter in necessity, sure,
a wise fighter,
but a professional?
One of los Generales?
Seems to me she has better things
to do than be a hero.
Medals were made for flatter chests.
They sort of dangle off her tits
and look embarrassing.
The uniforms don't fit.

If she shoots from the hip,
she hears the freudians applauding—
See? See? they say,
See? See? She wants one!
(She wants mine!
She can't have it!
She can't can she Daddy?
                              No, son.)

        Others say she's a goddess,
The Goddess, transcendent,
knowing everything by nature,
the Archetype
at the typewriter.
I resist that definition.

Her work, I really think her work
isn't fighting, isn't winning,
isn't being the Earth, isn't being the Moon.
Her work, I really think her work
is finding what her real work is
and doing it,
her work, her own work,
her being human,
her being in the world.

        So, if I am
a writer, my work
is words. Unwritten letters.

Words are my way of being
human, woman, me.

213

Word is the whorl that spins me,
the shuttle thrown through the warp of years
to weave a life, the hand
that shapes to use, to grace.
Word is my tooth,
my wing.
Word is my wisdom.

I am a bundle of letters
in a secret drawer
in an old desk.
What is in the letters?
What do they say?

     I am kept here a prisoner by the evil Duke.

     Georgie is much better now, and I have been canning peaches
     like mad.

     I cannot tell my husband or even my sister, I cannot live
     without you, I think of you day and night, when will you
     come to me?

     My brother Will hath gone to London and though I begg'd
     with all my heart to go with him nor he nor my Father
     would have it so, but laugh'd and said, Time the wench was
     married.

     The ghost of a woman walks in this house. I have heard her
     weeping in the room that was used as a nursery.

     If I only knew that my letters were reaching you, but there
     is no way to get information at any of the bureaus, they
     will not say where you have been sent.

Don't grieve for me. I know what I am doing.

Bring the kids and they can all play together and we can sit
and talk till we're blue in the face.

Did he know about her cousin Roger and the shotgun?

I don't know if it's any good but I've been working on
it ever since September.

How many of us will it take to hang him?

I am taking the family to America, the land of Freedom.

I have found a bundle of old letters in a secret compartment
in my desk.

Letters of words of stories:
they tell stories.
The writer tells stories, the stories,
over, and over, and over.

Man does, they say, and Woman is.
Doing and being. Do and be.
O.K., I be writing, Man.
I be telling.
("Je suis là où ça parle,"
says la belle Hélène.)
I be saying and parlaying.
I be being
this way. How do I do being?
Same way I be doing.
I would call it working,
or else, it doesn't matter, playing.

The writer at her work
is playing.
Not chess not poker not monopoly,
none of the war games—
Even if she plays by all their rules,
and wins—wins what?
Their funny money?—
not playing hero,
not playing god—
well, but listen, making things
is a kind of godly business, isn't it?—
All right, then, playing god:
Aphrodite the Maker, without whom
"nothing is born into the shining
borders of light, nor is anything lovely or lovable made,"
Spider Grandmother, spinning,
Thought Woman, making it all up,
Coyote Woman, playing—
playing it, a game,
without a winner or a loser,
a game of skill, a game of make
believe.

Sure it's a gamble,
but not for money.
Sorry Ernie this ain't stud.
The stakes
are a little higher.

        The writer at her work
is odd, is peculiar, is particular,
certainly, but not, I think,

singular.
She tends to the plural.

I for example am Ursula; Miss
Ursula Kroeber;
Mrs. then Ms. Le Guin;
Ursula K. Le Guin; this latter is
"the writer," but who were,
who are, the others?
She is the writer
at their work.

      What are they doing,
those plurals of her?
Lying in bed.
Lazy as hound dogs.
She-Plural is lying in bed
in the morning early.
Long before light, in winter;
in summer "the morning people
are chirping on the roof."
And like the sparrows
her thoughts go hopping
and flying and trying out words.
And like the light of morning
her thought impalpably touches
shape, and reveals it,
brings seeing from dimness,
being from inexhaustible chaos.

That is the good time.

That is the time when this she-plural writer
finds what is to be written.
In the first light,
seeing with the eyes
of the child waking,
lying between sleep and the day
in the body of dream,
in the body of flesh
that has been/is
a fetus, a baby, a child, a girl, a woman, a lover, a mother,
has contained other bodies,
incipient beings, minds unawakened, not to awaken,
has been sick, been damaged, been healed,
been old, is born and dying, will die,
in the mortal, inexhaustible
body
of her work:

That is the good time.

Spinning the fleece of the sun, that cloudy mass,
weaving a glance and a gesture,
shaping the clay of emotion;
housekeeping. Patterning.
Following patterns.
Lying there
in the dreamtime
following patterns.

    So then you have to cut it out—
take a deep breath,
the first cut, the blank page!—

and sew it together (drudgery,
toil in the sacred sweatshop)—
the garment, the soul-coat,
the thing made of words,
cloth of the sunfleece,
the new clothes of the Emperor.

(Yes, and some kid comes along
and yaps, "But he hasn't any clothes on!"
Muzzle the brat
till it learns
that none of us has any clothes on,
that our souls are naked,
dressed in words only,
in charity only,
the gift of the others.
Any fool can see through it.
Only fools say so.)

      Long ago when I was Ursula
writing, but not "the writer,"
and not very plural yet,
and worked with the owls not the sparrows,
being young, scribbling at midnight:

I came to a place
I couldn't see well in the darkness,
where the road turned
and divided, it seemed like,
going different ways.
I was lost.
I didn't know which way.

It looked like one roadsign said To Town
and the other didn't say anything.

So I took the way that didn't say.
I followed
myself.
"I don't care," I said,
terrified.
"I don't care if nobody ever reads it!
I'm going *this* way."

And I found myself
in the dark forest, in silence.

You maybe have to find yourself,
your selves,
in the dark forest.
Anyhow, I did then. And still now,
always. At the bad time.

　　　When you find the hidden catch
in the secret drawer
behind the false panel
inside the concealed compartment
in the desk in the attic
of the house in the dark forest,
and press the spring firmly,
a door flies open to reveal
a bundle of old letters,
and in one of them
is a map
of the forest

that you drew yourself
before you ever went there.

      The Writer at her Work:
I see her walking
on a path through a pathless forest,
or a maze, a labyrinth.
As she walks she spins,
and the fine thread falls behind her
following her way,
telling
where she is going,
where she has gone.
Telling the story.
The line, the thread of voice,
the sentences saying the way.

      The Writer on her Work:
I see her, too, I see her
lying on it.
Lying, in the morning early,
rather uncomfortable.
Trying to convince herself
that it's a bed of roses,
a bed of laurels,
or an innerspring mattress,
or anyhow a futon.
But she keeps twitching.

There's a *lump,* she says.
There's something
like a *rock*—like a *lentil*—

I can't sleep.

There's *something*
the size of a split pea
that I haven't written.
That I haven't written right.
I can't sleep.

She gets up
and writes it.
Her work
is never done.

NOTES ON CONTRIBUTORS

DIANE ACKERMAN was born in Waukegan, Illinois. She received her B.A. from Pennsylvania State University and several graduate degrees, including a doctorate, from Cornell University. Her five books of poetry include *The Planets: A Cosmic Pastoral*, a verse drama, *Reverse Thunder*, whose central figure is the seventeenth-century Mexican nun Sor Juana Inés de la Cruz, and *Jaguar of Sweet Laughter: New and Selected Poems*. Among her prose works are the memoirs *Twilight of the Tenderfoot* and *On Extended Wings*, as well as *A Natural History of the Senses* and the forthcoming *Bats, Crocs, Penguins and Albatrosses*. A staff writer for *The New Yorker*, she is at work on a second collection of natural history essays.

MARGARET ATWOOD was born in Ottawa, Ontario, in 1939 and was educated at the University of Toronto, Radcliffe College, and Harvard University. Her first novel, *The Edible Woman*, was published in 1969; she has since published eleven other novels, among them *Surfacing, Lady Oracle*, and most recently *Cat's Eye*. *Selected Poems II: Poems Selected and New 1976–1986* is her most recent poetry collection. Her many literary awards include a Guggenheim Fellowship; she is also a Fellow of the Royal Society of Canada, the holder of many honorary degrees, and has served as president of the Writers' Union of Canada. Her work has been translated into many languages and is the subject of several critical studies. Her novel *The Handmaid's Tale* was recently made into a feature film. She lives in Toronto with novelist Graeme Gibson and their daughter Jess.

ANITA DESAI's most recent novel is *Baumgartner's Bombay,* published by Knopf in 1989. Born of Bengali and German parents in 1937 in Mussoorie, India, she was educated in Delhi. Her novel *Clear Light of Day* was nominated for the Booker Prize (1980), as was *In Custody* (1984). *Fire on the Mountain* received both the Royal Society of Literature's Winifred Holtby Memorial Prize and the 1978 National Academy of Letters Award (Delhi). She has also written children's books and a book of short stories, *Games at Twilight.* A fellow of the Royal Society of Literature in London, she is also a Fellow of Girton College, Cambridge, and has taught writing at Smith College and Mount Holyoke College in the United States. Married with four children, she currently resides in South Hadley, Massachusetts.

HARRIET DOERR was born in Pasadena, California, in 1910; she has lived much of her life in Mexico and now resides in her hometown. Educated at Smith College and Stanford University in the late 1920s, she returned to Stanford in 1977 to earn a B.A. and do graduate work in fiction writing. With the help of a Wallace Stegner Fellowship at Stanford, she wrote her first novel, *Stones for Ibarra,* which is set in Mexico. It has won numerous awards, among them a National Book Award for a First Work of Fiction, and has also been adapted as a film for television. She has in recent years published stories in *The New Yorker* and *Atlantic,* and her story "Edie: A Life" appeared in the *O. Henry Awards Prize Stories* and *Best American Short Stories* (1989). She is currently working on a second novel, as yet untitled, also set in Mexico, "but not in Ibarra."

· · ·

Rita Dove, born in Akron, Ohio, in 1952, received her B.A. degree summa cum laude from Miami University (Ohio) and an M.F.A. from the University of Iowa Writers Workshop; she has also studied at the University of Tübingen in West Germany. Her poetry collections include *The Yellow House on the Corner* (1980), *Museum* (1983), *Thomas and Beulah* (1986), and *Grace Notes* (1989); several collections have been translated into German. She has been professor of English at Arizona State University, currently teaches at the University of Virginia, and is an associate editor of *Callaloo: A Journal of Afro-American and African Arts and Letters.* Her awards have included the Pulitzer Prize in Poetry (1987), Guggenheim and Fulbright Fellowships, and two National Endowment for the Arts Fellowships. The recipient of several honorary doctorates, she has also been a Portia Pittman Fellow in English at Tuskegee Institute. She is currently at work on a novel, *Through the Ivory Gate.* She is married to the German novelist Fred Viebahn and is the mother of a daughter, Aviva.

Gretel Ehrlich was born and raised in California and was educated at Bennington College, UCLA Film School, and the New School for Social Research. She now lives in Wyoming, where she writes and also works as a rancher. Her reflections on life in Wyoming have appeared in the short story collection *Wyoming Stories* and in book form in *The Solace of Open Spaces,* as well as in *The New York Times, Atlantic,* and *Harper's. To Touch the Water* (1981) was published by Ahsahta Press in the Modern and Contemporary Poets of the West Series. *Heart Mountain,* a novel about Japanese-Americans forced into a Wyoming relocation camp during the Second World War, was published in 1988. She has received awards from the National Endowment for the Arts, the Guggenheim Foundation, the American Academy of Arts and Letters, and, most recently, from the Whiting Foundation. She lives with her husband on their ranch in Shell, in northern Wyoming.

CAROLYN FORCHÉ's first collection of poetry, *Gathering the Tribes* (Yale University Press, 1976), won the Yale Series of Younger Poets Award. In 1977, after receiving a Guggenheim Fellowship, she went to El Salvador. Her experiences there led to her second book, *The Country Between Us* (Harper and Row, 1982), which was chosen as the Lamont Selection of the Academy of American Poets. Forché has traveled extensively, and has lived in Paris, Beirut, and South Africa. She translated Salvadoran poet and novelist Claribel Alegría's *Flores del Volcan* into English, and wrote the text for *El Salvador: Work of Thirty Photographers;* currently she is at work on a book-length poem tentatively titled *The Angel of History*. In 1991, W. W. Norton & Co. will publish her anthology of twentieth-century "poetry of witness." She has served as visiting lecturer at colleges and universities, and is now a member of the writing faculty at George Mason University in Virginia, where she lives with her husband and child.

KAYE GIBBONS lives in Raleigh, North Carolina, with her husband, Michael, and their three daughters. She was born in Nash County, North Carolina, in 1960, was graduated from Rocky Mount High School, and studied at North Carolina State University and the University of North Carolina at Chapel Hill. Her first novel, *Ellen Foster,* published by Algonquin Books in 1987, was awarded the Sue Kaufman Prize for First Fiction by the American Academy of Arts and Letters, and is now being developed for a motion picture. Her second novel, *A Virtuous Woman,* appeared in 1989. Both novels have been published throughout Europe, in several languages. In

1990, she received the PEN/Revson Award for Fiction. She is currently working on a third novel and a volume of literary criticism.

NATALIA GINZBURG's body of work in English translation includes the autobiographical novel *Family Sayings* and the novels *All Our Yesterdays* and *The City and the House.* A playwright and critic, she has also written a collection of essays, *The Little Virtues,* and the nonfiction work *Serena Cruz, or True Justice,* recently published in Italy. Born in Palermo in 1916, she grew up in Turin, where she worked as a publisher and writer. In 1938 she married Leone Ginzburg, and was active with him in anti-Fascist causes; they and their three children were confined by the Fascists in the Abruzzi region in the 1940s. In 1943 they went to Rome, where her husband was arrested by the Germans; he died in prison in 1944. After the war she became an editor at the publishing house Einaudi. She has translated Proust and Flaubert into Italian; she was also elected a senator in the Italian Parliament in 1983 and played a small role in Pasolini's *The Gospel According to Saint Matthew.* Her two sons are university professors and her daughter is a psychoanalyst. Since 1950, Ginzburg has lived in Rome.

PATRICIA HAMPL is a memoirist and poet; her memoir *A Romantic Education,* on her Czech heritage and her visit to Prague, won a Houghton Mifflin Literary Fellowship. Her poems and prose have appeared in such magazines and anthologies as *Antaeus, The Paris Review, The New Yorker, The New York Times Book Review,* and *Best American Short Stories.* She has published two books of poetry, *Woman Before an Aquarium* and *Resort and Other Poems.* In addition, she is the author of *Spillville,* a prose meditation on Antonín Dvořák's 1893 visit to a small Iowa farm town. She has received fellowships from the Guggenheim Foundation, the National Endowment for the Arts, the Bush Foundation, and the Ingram Merrill Foundation, among others, and is a recent recipient of a MacArthur Prize fellowship. She teaches at the University of Minnesota, and is now at work on a memoir about growing up Catholic. She lives with her husband in St. Paul, her hometown.

LINDA HOGAN is a Chickasaw poet, novelist, and essayist. Her poetry collection *Seeing Through the Sun* (1985) received an American Book Award from the Before Columbus Foundation. *Savings* (1988) is her most recent book of poetry; a first novel, *Mean Spirit,* was published in 1990 by Atheneum. She has received a National Endowment for the Arts grant, a Minnesota Arts Board grant, a Colorado Writer's Fellowship, and the Five Civilized Tribes Museum playwriting award. She is an associate professor at the University of Colorado, and is involved as a volunteer in the conservation and rehabilitation of birds of prey.

DIANE JOHNSON was born in 1934 in Moline, Illinois. She was educated at Stephens College and the University of Utah, and received her M.A. and Ph.D. from UCLA. Her novels include *Fair Game* (1965), *The Shadow Knows* (1974), and *Lying Low,* which was nominated for the National Book Award for Fiction in 1979. She has received a Guggenheim Fellowship (1977–78), as well as the Rosenthal Award and The Strauss Living from the American Academy of Arts and Letters (1979). Her nonfiction work includes *Lesser Lives: The Biography of the First Mrs. Meredith* (1972), the essay collection *Terrorists and Novelists* (1982), and *Dashiell Hammett: A Life* (1983). She has adapted *The Shadow Knows* as a screenplay and also the Stephen King novel *The Shining* in collaboration with writer/director Stanley Kubrick. A frequent contributor to *The*

New York Review of Books, she has been professor of English at the University of California at Davis. Her new novel, *Health and Happiness,* was published by Knopf in 1990. The mother of four grown children, she now divides her time between San Francisco and Paris, and is writing "a sort of travel book in which the heroine of *Persian Nights* sees something more of the world."

ELIZABETH JOLLEY was born in 1923 near Birmingham, England, of Austrian-British parentage. Educated in a Quaker boarding school, she served as a nurse in the Second World War. In 1959 she emigrated to Western Australia, where she now lives with her husband, Leonard. She teaches at the Curtin University of Technology, conducts writing workshops in remote country areas and in prisons, and raises geese and fruit trees on a small rural farm. Her first book, *The Five Acre Virgin and Other Stories,* appeared in 1976; since then she has published twelve books, among them the novels *Foxybaby* (1985), *The Sugar Mother* (1988), and, most recently, *My Father's Moon* (1989) and *Cabin Fever* (1990), as well as a number of plays for radio. Her works have been translated into German, French, Spanish, and Russian; among her many honors, she was the 1988 recipient of the Canada/Australia Literary Prize. The title for her essay in this collection is a quote from Alexander Pope.

MAXINE KUMIN was born in Philadelphia in 1925 and received her bachelor's and master's degrees at Radcliffe College. The mother of three children, she was first a writer of light verse and of children's books; she then went on to publish nine books of poetry, beginning with *Halfway* (1961). Among her other titles are *Up Country,* which received the Pulitzer Prize for Poetry in 1973, *Our Ground Time Here Will Be Brief: New and Selected Poems* (1982), and most recently *Nurture* (1989). She has also written four novels, a short story collection, and two books of essays. The recipient of many awards and honorary degrees, she has been a Consultant in Poetry for the Library of Congress and a Fellow of the Mary Ingraham Bunting Institute at Radcliffe College; she also received an Academy of American Poets Fellowship in 1985. She has lectured and taught widely at universities, including Columbia University, Princeton University, and M.I.T., and has been a staff member at the Bread Loaf Writers' Conference. She lives with her husband on a two-hundred-acre farm in central New Hampshire where they raise horses.

URSULA K. LE GUIN was born in 1929 in Berkeley, California, daughter of writer Theodora Kroeber and anthropologist Alfred L. Kroeber. Educated at Radcliffe College and Columbia University, she has received several Hugo and Nebula awards for her speculative fiction, including *The Left Hand of Darkness* (1969) and *The Dispossessed* (1974). *The Farthest Shore* (1972) won a National Book Award. In addition to her fifteen novels, she has published four volumes of short stories, as well as a screenplay (*King Dog,* 1985), children's books, poetry, and collections of critical essays. Her most recent collection of stories is *Buffalo Gals* (1987). Married to historian Charles A. Le Guin in 1953, she is the mother of three grown children; she presently lives in Oregon.

JAN MORRIS was born in 1926, was educated at Oxford, and is a Fellow of the Royal Society of Literature and of the Academi Cymreig, the Welsh academy of literature. She divides her time between her library-house in North Wales, her *dacha* in the Black Mountains of South Wales, and travel abroad. Her best-known books include the *Pax Britannica* trilogy about the British Empire, studies of Wales, Venice, Oxford, Manhattan, and Hong Kong, six volumes of collected travel essays, and a novel, *Last Letters from Hav,* which was shortlisted for the Booker Prize in London in 1985. She has also written two autobiographical volumes, *Conundrum,* which described her mid-life change of sexual role, and the more recent *Pleasures of a Tangled Life.* She edited the *Oxford Book of Oxford,* is now writing a book about the city of Sydney, and is shortly to edit the collected travel writings of Virginia Woolf.

BHARATI MUKHERJEE was born in Calcutta and lived in Canada with her husband, writer Clark Blaise, before emigrating to the United States. She attended college in India and also the University of Iowa, where she received an M.F.A. and Ph.D. She won the National Book Critics Circle Award in fiction for *The Middleman and Other Stories,* becoming the first naturalized American citizen to do so. Her other writings include *Darkness* (1985), a collection of stories; *Days and Nights in Calcutta,* a travel memoir co-authored with her husband; and a novel, *Jasmine* (1989). At Emory University in Atlanta she was writer-in-residence in 1984; she has also taught creative writing at Columbia University, New York University, and Queens College, and is now a professor in the English Department of the University of California at Berkeley. She and her husband have two grown sons.

ELENA PONIATOWSKA, daughter of a Mexican mother (Paula de Amor) and Polish father, was born in Paris in 1933 and returned to Mexico as a young girl. She began her career as a journalist in 1954, becoming the first woman to receive Mexico's National Journalism Award in 1977. Among her books that incorporate interviews are *Massacre in Mexico,* an account of the 1968 Mexican student movement, as well as her major work of testimonial literature, *Hasta no verte Jesús mío* (1969), a novel telling the life story of Jesusa, a

Mexican peasant woman, from her involvement in the Mexican
Revolution to her life in contemporary Mexico. Her epistolary
novel *Dear Diego* (1978), translated into English, is the romance of a
young Russian woman and the painter Diego Rivera. After the 1985
Mexico City earthquake, she wrote about its effects and played a
major role in organizing relief efforts; her political activities currently are centered on the city's housing situation. She has three
children and was married to Guillermo Haro, a Mexican astronomer
who died in 1987.

JANET STERNBURG was born in Boston, Massachusetts, and received a
degree in philosophy from the New School for Social Research in
New York. A poet and essayist, as well as writer for theater and film,
she has a special interest in women and creativity. This is the second
collection of essays that she has edited on being a woman and a
writer; the first *The Writer on Her Work* appeared in 1980. For film,
she has produced and directed the award-winning public television
portrait *Virginia Woolf: The Moment Whole;* for theater, she has
adapted and staged the works of Colette, Louise Bogan, H.D., and
Isak Dinesen for the Manhattan Theatre Club, where she served as
director of the Writers in Performance series. Her work on and
about other artists also includes the films *El Teatro Campesino* and
Thomas Eakins: A Motion Portrait, as well as the series *Likely Stories.*
Her poems and essays have been widely published in anthologies and
journals, and she has received a scriptwriting award from the National Endowment for the Humanities. Married to college president
Steven Lavine, she divides her time between New York, where she
serves as media consultant to the Rockefeller Foundation, and Los
Angeles, where she teaches creative writing at the California Institute of the Arts. She is currently curating a television series of films
by women and working on a collection of her personal essays.

· · ·

LUISA VALENZUELA was born in Buenos Aires in 1938. At age nineteen she published her first short story in *Ficción,* a Buenos Aires literary magazine. At twenty-one she wrote her first novel, *Clara.* She first came to the United States in 1969–70 through the International Writers Workshop at the University of Iowa. She has taught creative writing through the English Department of New York University, and is a Fellow of the New York Institute of the Humanities and of the Fund for Free Expression. She received a Guggenheim Fellowship in 1983. Her work in English translation includes *Clara: Thirteen Stories and a Novel* (1976); *Strange Things Happen Here* (1978); *The Lizard's Tail* (1983), a novel; and the short story collection *Open Door* (1988). Forthcoming are the novels *Cat O'Nine Deaths* and *Black Novel with Argentines.* She has lived abroad in Paris and in Mexico, and most recently, from 1979 to 1989, in New York. She recently returned to Argentina where she is at work on a novel and a play, *Realidad nacional desde la cama.*

JOY WILLIAMS grew up in Maine and now lives in Arizona and Florida. She has written three novels—*State of Grace* (nonimated for the 1974 National Book Award), *The Changeling* (1978), and *Breaking and Entering* (1988)—and two collections of stories—*Taking Care* (1982) and *Escapes* (1990)—as well as a guide to the Florida Keys and essays on the environment, hunting, sharks, and the electric chair. Her fiction has appeared in *Esquire, Granta,* and *The Paris Review* and is frequently anthologized in *Best American Short Stories.* In 1989 she received an award from the American Academy of Arts and Letters.

ACKNOWLEDGMENTS

The quote from Louise Bogan is from *A Poet's Alphabet,* McGraw-Hill, 1970, p. 420. Reprinted with permission of Ruth Limmer, Trustee of the Estate of Louise Bogan.

Natalia Ginzburg, "My Vocation," reprinted from *The Little Virtues* by Natalia Ginzburg, copyright © 1962 by Giulio Einaudi s.p.a., Turin, translation copyright © 1985 by Dick Davis, published by Seaver Books, New York, 1986, and reprinted with permission of Seaver Books and Carcanet Press, Limited.

Maxine Kumin, "Nightmare," the poem from *Halfway,* is reprinted in *Our Ground Time Here Will Be Brief,* Penguin 1982, and appears with permission of Viking Penguin, Inc., New York.